EazyChinese

CW01502028

易达汉语系列教材
EazyChinese Textbook Series

MAGICAL CHINESE CHARACTERS

汉字部首教程

Radicals for Learning Chinese Characters

主编：达世平、达婉中
Chief Authors: Da Shiping, Wendy Da

北京语言大学出版社
BEIJING LANGUAGE AND CULTURE
UNIVERSITY PRESS

图书在版编目 (CIP) 数据

汉字部首教程.1/达世平，达婉中主编；易达汉语编
辑委员会编.—北京：北京语言大学出版社，2008.3
　（易达汉语系列教材）
ISBN 978 - 7 - 5619 - 2022 - 0

Ⅰ．汉…　Ⅱ．①达…②达…③易　Ⅲ．汉字 – 部首 – 对
外汉语教学 – 教材　Ⅳ．H195.4

中国版本图书馆 CIP 数据核字（2008）第 016335 号

书　　名	汉字部首教程·1
责任印制	汪学发

出版发行：**北京语言大学出版社**

社　　址	北京市海淀区学院路 15 号　邮政编码：100083
网　　址	www.blcup.com
电　　话	发行部　82303650/3591/3651
	编辑部　82303647
	读者服务部　82303653/3908
印　　刷	北京新丰印刷厂
经　　销	全国新华书店

版　　次	2008 年 3 月第 1 版　2008 年 3 月第 1 次印刷
开　　本	889 毫米×1194 毫米　1/16　印张：11.5
字　　数	122 千字　印数：1 - 3000 册
书　　号	ISBN 978 - 7 - 5619 - 2022 - 0/H·08011
定　　价	46.00 元

凡有印装质量问题，本社负责调换。电话：82303590

　　学完《汉字字母教程》以后，就有了一个很好的汉字基础，可以进入汉字学习的第二阶段了。在这个阶段中，将要学习大约 1000 个合体字。

　　合体字是由两个或两个以上的"字母"（即核心汉字）组成的，所以，合体字是可以分割的。在全部汉字中，合体字占 90% 以上，其中，绝大多数是形声字。所谓形声字，就是这类合体字可以分成两部分，一部分是"形"，表示意义，另一部分是"声"，表示读音。形声字中表示意义的那部分通常称为部首，而表示读音的那部分通常称为声旁。

　　我们从《汉字字母教程》中挑选了最常用的、能够在合体字中做部首表示意义的字母，如"女"、"木"、"车"等，又增加了一些在现代汉字中已经不能独立成字而只能做部首的字母，如"辶"、"艹"、"宀"等，把这些部首作为每一课的中心，并学习由这些部首组成的若干合体字。从中可以发现，学习这些合体汉字已经不难了，因为，相同的部首，通常有相似的意思；同时也会发现，不用每个汉字都抄写很多遍，因为，大多数的"字母"以前已经学过了，现在，只要把它们拼合起来就行了。这样，就可以很快学会很多汉字。

　　生字表中的数字"①、②、③、④"表示在《汉字等级大纲》中的等级，如"①"级为最常用字。

　　为了强调部首学习，加快利用部首集中识字，我们在编写每课课文时，有意把由本课部首构成的汉字集中编进课文，但是，由于课文内容和长度的限制，还是有很多由本课部首构成的常用汉字没有出现，只能出现在其他课的课文中。这对于学习者按照部首会聚生字不太方便。因此，我们建议，在学习这本教材的同时，使用《易达汉语系列教材》中的《我的部首小字典》。《我的部首小字典》是一本字典型的练习册，包含了122个常用部首，要求使用者把自己学过的汉字填写在各个部首下面的空格中，特别适合配合《汉字部首教程》使用。

PREFACE

After finishing *Magical Chinese Characters — Building Blocks for Learning Chinese Characters*, you've already had a good foundation for learning Chinese characters. Now you are ready to move on to the second stage, during which you will learn about 1000 compound characters.

Compound characters are composed of two or more building blocks (core characters), implying that they can be separable. More than 90% of the Chinese characters are of this kind, among which most are pictophonetic in structure, with half of the character, namely the radical, expressing the meaning, and the other half indicating the sound.

We have chosen from the *Building Blocks for Learning Chinese Characters* the most commonly-used building blocks which can be used as radicals expressing meaning in compound characters, such as "女", "木", "车", etc., and radicals which do not by themselves occur as characters in modern Chinese, such as "辶", "艹", "宀", etc. These radicals will comprise the focuses of our lessons, and you will learn some compound characters composed of them. You will find it not difficult to learn these characters, because the characters with the same radical usually have similar meanings. You will also notice that there is much less character-writing practice because you've already mastered the building blocks — all you have to do now is to put them together into different combinations. This way you can make significant progress in your character learning.

In vocabulary, the numbers "①, ②, ③ and ④" correspond with the four levels in *Guideline for Chinese Words and Characters*, with "①" representing the most commonly-used characters.

In order to emphasize the learning of radicals and characters, in each lesson we deliberately put the characters made up of the radicals learned in current lesson into the text. However, due to the limited content and length of the article, many newly-learned characters can't be included in the current lesson but have to occur in other lessons, which causes a lot of inconvenience for the learners. Therefore, we suggest learners to use at the same time *My Mini Radical Dictionary* in the same *EazyChinese Textbooks Series* since as a dictionary-type workbook with 122 commonly-used radicals, it enables the learners to fill in the characters they've learned in the blanks corresponding with the constituent radicals, which is very suitable to be used together with this *Radicals for Learning Chinese Characters*.

CONTENTS 目录

i

UNIT

1

第1单元

与人有关
Human Related

第1课 人部 Human ◎1

■ 课文 TEXT

伯比健身

　　伯比是俄罗斯人，他觉得中国和俄罗斯都是伟大的民

族。为了促进两国的文化交流，去年八月份，他以文化大

使的身份到中国来工作，住在位于上海市西南的一个朋

友的家里。为了使自己的身体保持健康，双休日的时候，

他就同伙伴们一起去跑步，从来也没有停止过。他认为

任何事都没有身体重要，并且认为，跑步是最方便的运

动方法。他经常给他的伯父写信，叫伯父也像他一样多

做体育运动，当然更要学会保护自己，不要摔倒，不要

受伤。

■ 部首 RADICAL 人（亻）rén

★ The character originally looked like a person standing. Used as a radical, it is related to human being's action, behavior, temperament, etc. When written on the left as a human-related radical, it is changed to "亻", which is called "dānrénpáng". It is also used as a sound part.

■ 书写 WRITING

丿 亻

亻							亻

■ 生字 NEW CHARACTERS

课文中的亻部字

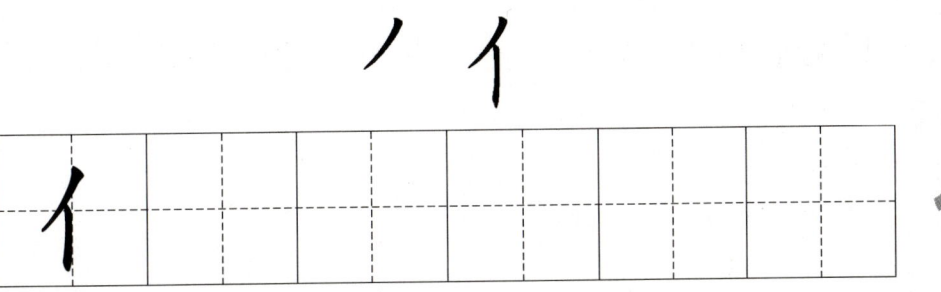

伴	③ bàn *n.* companion, partner；*v.* accompany 伙伴 fellow, partner　老伴儿 old husband or wife ★ 伴 and 半 have the same pronunciation.	伴
保	② bǎo *v.* keep, protect　保卫 safeguard 保持(chí) keep　保护(hù) protect　保安(ān) guard ★ Originally it represented a person holding a baby.	保
便	① biàn *adj.* convenient；pián　便宜(yi) cheap 方便 convenience　随(suí)便 informal, anyhow, at will 大便 defecate, shit, stool　小便 pee, piss, urinate	便

伯 ✓	② bó　*n.* uncle, father's elder brother 伯伯 uncle　　伯父 father's elder brother ★ 伯 and 白 have the same beginning sound b.	伯		
促	② cù　*v.* promote, urge 促进 promote, advance ★ 促 and 足 have the same ending sound u.	促		
倒	① dǎo　*v.* fall over, tumble down; dào　*v.* upside down 摔(shuāi) 倒 have a fall ★ 倒 and 到 have the same pronunciation.	倒		
俄	③ é 俄罗(luó)斯(sī) Russia ★ 俄 and 我 had the same sound in ancient times.	俄		
份 ✓	② fèn　*n.* share, portion 身份 identity　　以……身份 according to, as ★ 份 and 分(fēn, Lesson 46) differ only in tone.	份		
何 ✓	① hé　*pron.* what; same sound as 和 任何 any　　为何 why ★ 何 and 可 have the same ending sound e.	何		
候	① hòu　*v.* await; *n.* time 时候 moment, time	候		
化	① huà　*v.* change, burn up, -ize, -fy; similar to 比 文化 culture, civilization　　变(biàn)化 change ★ Originally it meant changing from dead.	化		
伙 ✓	② huǒ　*n.* mess, group 伙伴 fellow, partner, friend　　大伙儿 everybody, all ★ 伙 and 火 have the same pronunciation.	伙		
健 ✓	① jiàn　*adj.* healthy 健康(kāng) health ★ 健 and 建(jiàn) have the same pronunciation.	健		

任	① rèn *v.* assume somebody to a post, let similar to 王, 住	任		
	任何 any 任务 task, assignment			
	★ 任 and 壬 (rén) differ only in tone.			
伤	(傷) ② shāng *n., v.* injure	伤		
	similar to 每 and 力; same sound as 商			
	受(shòu)伤 be injured 伤心 sad, grieved			
使	① shǐ *v.* let, send, use; similar to 便	使		
	大使 ambassador			
	★ Originally it meant ambassador or serving as an envoy abroad. 史 and 吏 had the same sound in ancient times.			
体 ✓	(體) ① tǐ *n.* body, part of the body; similar to 休	体		
	身体 body 体育(yù) sports			
	★ It means "self".			
停	① tíng *v.* stop; similar to 亮	停		
	停下 stop 停止 stop			
	★ 停 and 亭(tíng) have the same pronunciation.			
伟	① wěi *adj.* big, great	伟		
	伟大 great, mighty			
	★ Originally it meant a big person. 伟 and 韦 (wéi) differ only in tone.			
位 ✓	① wèi *v.* locate; *mw [polite measure word for person]* same sound as 卫	位		
	位子 seat 位于 locate			
	★ It means the place where a person is standing.			
像	① xiàng *n.* portrait; *adj.* alike; same sound as 向	像		
	好像 seem, be like 像……一样 as, like			
	★ The portrait is like a person. 像 and 象 have the same pronunciation.			
信 ✓	① xìn *v.* believe; *n.* faith, letter	信		
	相信 believe 写信 write a letter 信心 confidence			
	★ A person should do what he said, and write down his words.			
休 ✓	① xiū *v.* stop (working or learning); similar to 体	休		
	休息(xi) rest, have a day off 双休日 two-day weekend			
	★ Originally it meant "stop working, sit under a tree and have a rest".			

| 住
✓ | ① zhù　*v.* live, stay, stop

★ 住 and 主 differ only in tone. | 住 | | |

课文中的其他生字

| 市 | ① shì *n.* city, town, market；same sound as 是 and 事
城市 city, town　　市场 (chǎng) market
超 (chāo)市 supermarket
★ The market was larger and larger and became a town or city. | 市 | | |
| 族 | ① zú　*n.* clan, race, group；same sound as 足
民族 nation, nationality
★ It originally looked like the weapon (arrow) gathered under the flag of national symbol. | 族 | | |

■ 书写 WRITING

亻 亻 俨 伫 伫 俟 侯 候							
候							

候

亻 化						
化						

化

亻 仁 仟 任						
任						

任

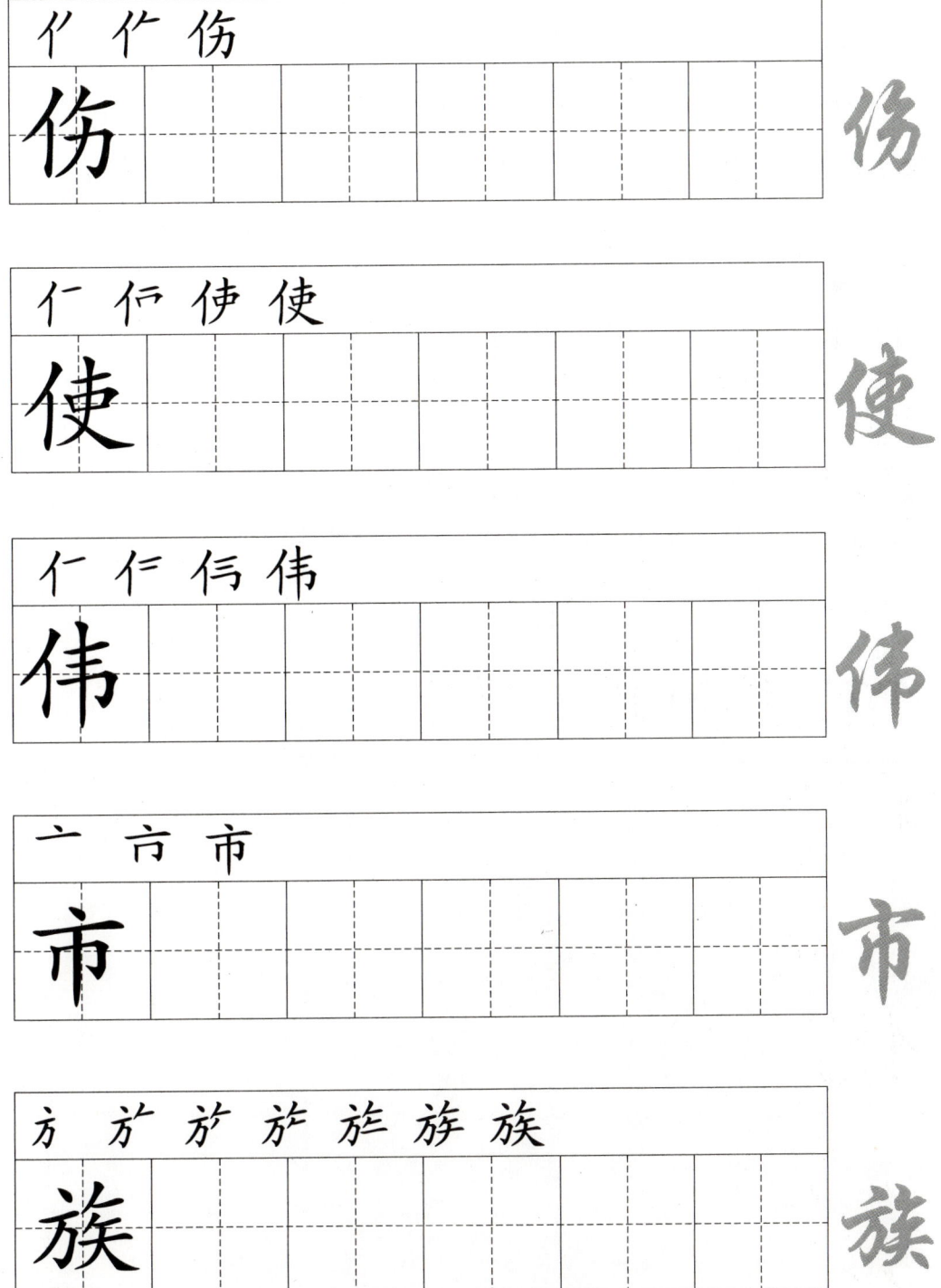

伤

使

伟

市

族

书写以前学过的字 Writing the characters you have learned before

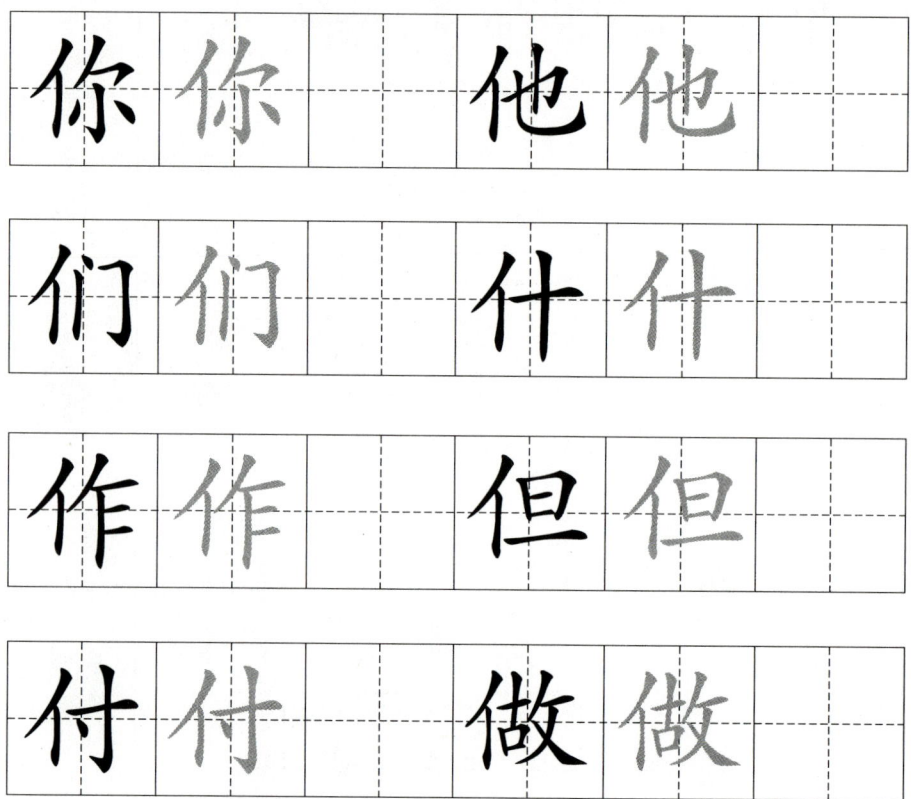

第2课 女部 Woman 🔘2

课文 TEXT

姜家姐妹

　　她姓姜，今年25岁，别人都叫她姜小姐。大学毕业后，她在一家妇女健身俱乐部工作。开始的时候，她工作很努力，把吃奶的力气都用出来了，可是工作还是干不好。后来，她的师傅对她说："干活不能光用力气，还要会动脑子、会安排时间；一个人要会工作、会休息、会学习、会娱乐。"说来真奇妙，从那以后，她仿佛换了一个人：工作越干越好，而且，还有很多休息与娱乐的时间。

　　姜小姐有一个姐姐和一个妹妹。姜小姐的姐姐已经结婚了，嫁到了一个姓姚的人家。姐姐刚生了一个孩子，丈夫请了一个阿姨，帮妻子照顾婴儿。婆婆对儿媳妇很好，也经常帮忙。姐姐的婚姻很幸福。姜小姐的妹妹还在上中学，是个可爱的小姑娘。

9

■ 部首 RADICAL 女 nǔ

★ The character originally looked like a woman with large chest kneeling (sitting in ancient times). Used as a radical, it is related to woman, and attributes associated with woman such as feature, shape, dressing up, family name, marriage, bearing, etc. Because women were looked down in ancient times, it also means bad temperament. It's usually written on the left or at the bottom.

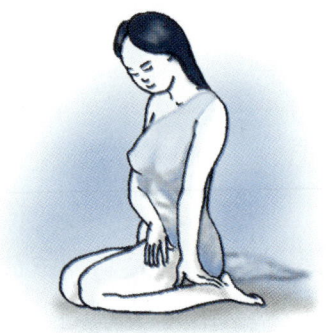

■ 生字 NEW CHARACTERS

课文中的女部字

妇	(婦) ② fù *n.* married woman, woman; same sound as 父 妇女 woman 夫 (fū) 妇 couple ★ The right part was a broom. It means the woman doing housework.	妇
姑	① gū *n.* aunt 姑妈 father's sister 姑娘 girl ★ 姑 and 古 differ only in tone.	姑
婚	② hūn *n.* marry, wedding; similar to 民 结 (jié) 婚 marriage ★ It was originally associated to a man marrying. 婚 and 昏 (hūn, Lesson 17) have the same pronunciation.	婚
嫁	③ jià *v.* marry, wed 出嫁 get married 嫁给 marry (sb.) ★ It was originally associated to a woman marrying. 嫁 and 家 differ only in tone.	嫁
姜	④ jiāng *n.* family name 姜先生 Mr. Jiang ★ 姜 and 羊 have the same ending sound iang.	姜

姐	① jiě *n.* elder sister 小姐 miss 姐姐 elder sister ★ 姐 and 且 have the same ending sound ie.	姐		
妹	① mèi *n.* younger sister；similar to 木 and 味 妹妹 younger sister 姐妹 sister ★ 妹 and 未 (wèi, Lesson 28) have the same ending sound ei.	妹		
妙	② miào *adj.* excellent 奇妙 wonderful 美妙 excellent, sweet ★The best age for woman is when they are young.	妙		
奶	① nǎi *n.* breast, milk；similar to 及 奶奶 grandma 牛奶 milk ★ 奶 and 乃(nǎi) have the same pronunciation.	奶		
娘	① niáng *n.* mum 姑娘(niang) girl, miss ★ 娘 and 良 have the same ending sound iang.	娘		
婆	③ pó *n.* mother-in-law, old woman 婆婆 mother-in-law 外婆 mother's mother ★ 婆 and 波 have the same ending sound o.	婆		
妻	② qī *n.* wife；same sound as 七 妻子 wife 夫 (fū)妻 couple ★It was originally like a hand (on the top) grasping a woman, later it came to mean female servant.	妻		
始	① shǐ *v.* begin；same sound as 史 and 使 开始 begin ★ It means the new life begins with a newborn baby.	始		
媳	② xí *n.* daughter-in-law 媳妇 daughter-in-law ★ 媳 and 息 differ only in tone.	媳		
姓	① xìng *n.* surname；*v.* be surnamed ★It means "born by women". In ancient times, the family name descended from the mother because children knew only their mother but not their father. 姓 and 生 had the same pronunciation in ancient times.	姓		

姚	yáo　*n.* family name; similar to 北 姚先生 Mr. Yao ★ 姚 and 兆 (zhào) have the same ending sound ao.	姚		
姨	② yí　*n.* aunt, mother's sister 阿(ā)姨 aunt, mother's sister, baby-sister, house-keeper ★ 姨 and 夷 (yí) have the same sound.	姨		
姻	② yīn　*n.* marriage 婚姻 marriage ★ 姻 and 因 have the same sound.	姻		
婴	(嬰) ③ yīng　*n.* baby, infant 婴儿 baby ★ The top part double "贝" means the baby had a necklace made of shells.	婴		
娱	(娛) ③ yú　*adj.* amusing; *v.* give pleasure to same sound as 鱼, 于 and 余　　娱乐 amusement ★Originally it meant making love with a woman. 娱 and 吴 (wú) have the similar sound.	娱		

课文中的其他生字

毕	(畢) ② bì　*v.* finish; same sound as 必 similar to 比 and 十　　毕业 graduate, finish school ★ 毕 and 比 differ only in tone.	毕		
仿	② fǎng　*v.* copy, imitate 模(mó)仿 imitate, copy ★ 仿 and 方 differ only in tone.	仿		
佛	② fú; fó　*n.* Buddha 仿佛 as if, be alike　　佛教 (jiào) Buddhism ★ 佛 and 弗 (fú) have the same sound.	佛		
傅	① fù　*n.* teacher; same sound as 付 师(shī)傅 master worker, teacher, mentor ★ 傅 and 甫 (fǔ) differ only in tone.	傅		

| 俱 | ② jù *adv.* all；similar to 其

俱乐部（bù）club

★ 俱 and 具 (jù) have the same pronunciation. | 俱 | | |

生词 NEW WORDS

奇妙：wonderful, marvelous

书写 WRITING

奼 妇 妇						
妇						

妇

奶 奶						
奶						

奶

一 ラ 手 手 妻 妻						
妻						

妻

奼 奼 始						
始						

始

姚 妈 妈 妈 姚 姚 姚

姚

姚

姨 女 妇 妈 姨 姨

姨

姨

佛 亻 亻 佛 佛

佛

佛

傅 亻 亻 亻 佴 佴 傅 傅

傅

傅

俱 亻 们 佴 佴 俱 俱

俱

俱

书写以前学过的字 Writing the characters you have learned before

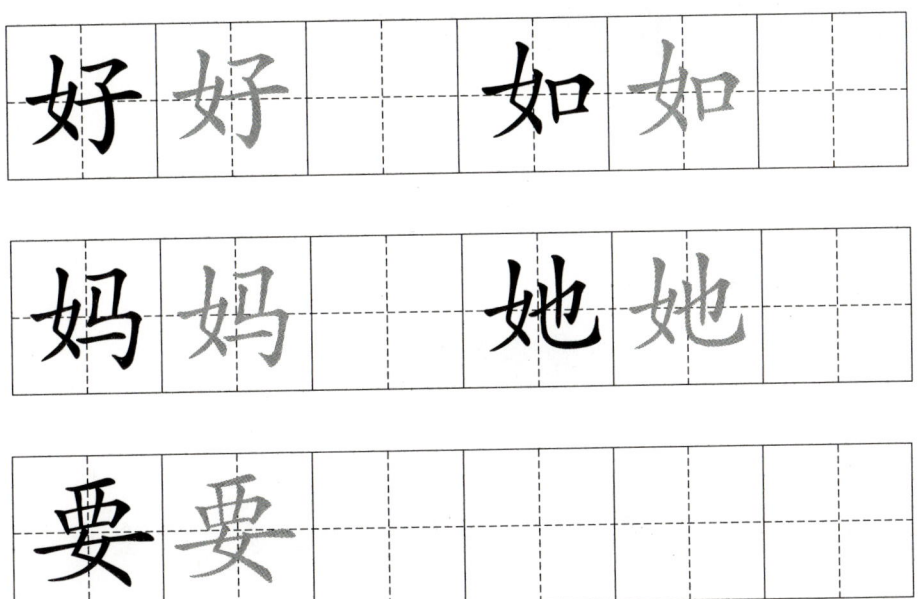

■ 课文 TEXT

有病就医

_{yī}

人要经常参加体育运动，身体才会健康，才会少生

病，还能保持优美的身材和充足的精力。人不能太胖，

也不能太瘦。太胖了活动不方便，太瘦了也不健康。工

作和学习不要太累，觉得疲倦了，就要伸伸腿、弯弯腰，

休息一下。俗话说：身体是革命的本钱。如果有了疾病，

就要去医院治疗。告诉医生什么地方痒、什么地方疼痛，

有没有痰等。如果得了很重的病，就要开刀动手术，虽然

会留下一些疤痕，但只要身体好了就行。

部首 RADICAL 疒 nè

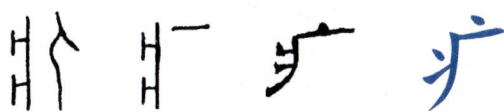

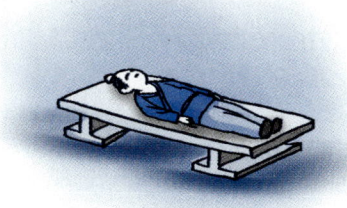

★ The character originally looked like a person lying on the bed, being sick. Used as a radical, it is related to illness and feeling of the body. It is usually written outside and called "bìngzìtóu".

书写 WRITING

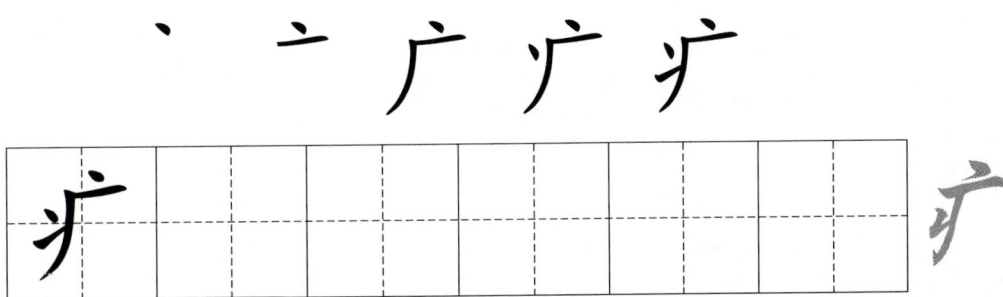

疒								疒

生字 NEW CHARACTERS

课文中的疒部字

疤	④ bā *n.* scar; similar to 把 and 爸; same sound as 八 伤疤 scar ★ 疤 and 巴 have the same pronunciation.	疤	
病	① bìng *v.* be ill; *n.* sickness; same sound as 并 生病 be sick 病人 patient ★ 病 and 丙 differ only in tone.	病	
痕	③ hén *n.* scar, mark; similar to 很 伤痕 scar 疤痕 scar ★ 痕 and 艮(gèn) have the same ending sound en.	痕	

疾	③ jí　*n.* disease, illness；similar to 失 疾病 disease, illness ★ Originally it meant coming down with an illness being shot by an arrow.	疾		
疗	（療）③ liáo　*v.* cure, treat 治(zhì)疗 cure ★ 疗 and 了(liǎo) differ only in tone.	疗		
疲	② pí　*adj.* tired 疲劳(láo) tired　　疲倦 tiredness ★ 疲 and 皮 have the same pronunciation.	疲		
瘦	② shòu　*adj.* emaciated, thin The antonym of 瘦 is 胖. ★ 瘦 and 叟(sǒu) have the same ending sound ou.	瘦		
痰	④ tán　*n.* phlegm, sputum; similar to 火 吐痰 spit, expectorate ★ 痰 and 炎(yán) have the same ending sound an.	痰		
疼	① téng　*adj.* pain 心疼 feel distressed, love dearly　头疼 headache 止疼药(yào) painkiller ★ 疼 and 冬 (dōng, Lesson 21) had similar sound in ancient times.	疼		
痛	① tòng　*adj.* ache, pain; similar to 用 头痛 headache　　止痛药(yào) painkiller 痛心 be distressed ★ 痛 and 甬(yǒng) have the same ending sound ong.	痛		
痒	（癢）④ yǎng　*adj.* itch, tickle ★ 痒 and 羊 differ only in tone.	痒		

课文中的其他生字

| 参 | （參）① cān　*v.* join
参加(jiā) join, attend, take part in
参观 (guān) visit, see | 参 | | |

充	② chōng v. stuff, charge, fill 充当 serve, act as 充足 enough, adequate, sufficient 充满(mǎn) be full of	充		
供	② gōng v. supply, provide; gòng n. offerings 提(tí)供 offer, provide 供养 make offerings to ★ 供 and 共 have the same pronunciation.	供		
估	② gū v. estimate 估计(jì) estimate 低估 underestimate ★ 估 and 古 differ only in tone.	估		
加	① jiā v. add, plus 参加 join, attend, take part in	加		
倦	③ juàn adj. tired 疲倦 tiredness ★ 倦 and 卷(juǎn) differ only in tone.	倦		
伸	② shēn v. extend, stretch 延(yán)伸 extend ★ 伸 and 申(shēn) have the same pronunciation.	伸		
受	② shòu v. accept, bear; similar to 学 and 觉 受伤 be injured, be wounded ★ The top and the bottom are both hands, meaning accepting things from the other's hand.	受		
俗	② sú n. custom; adj. common 俗话 common saying 风俗 custom ★ 俗 and 谷 have the same ending sound u.	俗		
弯	(彎) ② wān adj. curved; v. bend; n. turn 弯曲 bend, curve 弯腰 bow down, stoop ★ "弓" will be bent after it is drawn out for a shoot. 弯 and 峦(luán) have the same ending sound uɑn.	弯		
优	(優) ② yōu adj. excellent 优美 graceful, fine 优点 merit, advantage ★ 优 and 尤 differ only in tone.	优		

| 院 | ① yuàn *n.* yard 医(yī)院 hospital 学院 college 电影(yǐng)院 cinema, theater ★The left part means place. 院 and 完 (wán) have the same ending sound an. | 院 | | |

■ 书写 WRITING

疒 疒 疒 疾 疾						
疾						

疾

疒 疒 疒 疒 疒 疒 瘦 瘦							
瘦							

瘦

疒 疒 痛					
痛					

痛

ㄥ ㄙ 夬 叁 叁 参						
参						

参

、 一 云 云 充						
充						

充

亻 亻 亇 亇 伴 佚 佚 倦						
倦						

倦

亻 佀 伸						
伸						

伸

丶 丶 ⺈ ⺥ 𭅺 𢪘 受						
受						

受

亠 六 亦 亦 弯						
弯						

弯

■ 课文 TEXT

shì shi
一起来试试

你知道有一句话叫"病从口入"吗？就是说很多疾

病是从嘴巴开始的，这些疾病占了很大的比例。所以

吃东西要注意卫生，吃水果要先洗干净，味道变了的东

西就不要吃了，这样身体才会健康。大声喊叫、大声唱

歌和哈哈大笑对身体也有好处，可以使呼吸量更大。不

过，大声喊叫和唱歌要注意保护嗓子，更不能影响别人。

哪些地方比较好呢？告诉你吧：森林里、山里、田野上

特别好。咱们一起来试试吧！啊……

■ 部首 RADICAL 口 kǒu

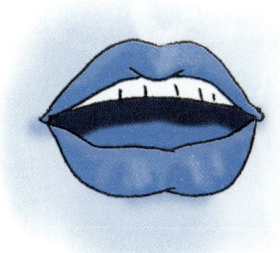

★ The character originally looked like a mouth opened. Used as a radical, it is related to mouth, language, action with mouth, voice, onomatopoeia or particle words, etc.

■ 生字 NEW CHARACTERS

课文中的口部字

啊	① ā, á, ǎ, à *int.* a *aux.* [*particle indicating mood*] ★ 啊 and 阿(ā) have the same pronunciation.	啊
吧	① ba [*particle indicating mood*]; similar to 把, 爸 and 疤 好吧 OK ★ 吧 and 巴 differ only in tone.	吧
唱	① chàng *v.* sing 唱歌 sing a song ★ 唱 and 昌(chāng) differ only in tone.	唱
告	gào *v.* tell, accuse 告诉(su) tell 报(bào)告 report ★ The top part is changed from 牛, meaning praying to the ancestors with ox.	告
哈	① hā *onomatopoeia* sound of laughing 哈哈 sound of laughing 马大哈 careless person ★ 哈 and 合 have the same beginning sound h.	哈
喊	① hǎn *v.* shout, call; similar to 成 喊叫 shout, cry out, yell ★ 喊 and 咸(xián) have the same ending sound an.	喊

呼	② hū　*v.* breathe out, call 呼吸 breath　　打招呼(dǎ zhāohu) greet sb. ★ 呼 and 乎 have the same pronunciation.	呼		
句	① jù　*n.* sentence same sound as 俱；similar to 可 and 包 句子 sentence　句号(hào) full stop　一句话 a sentence	句		
啦	① lā; la [*particle indicating mood*] same as "了啊" ★ 啦 and 拉(lā, Lesson 11) have the same pronunciation.	啦		
呢	① ne [*particle indicating mood*] 你呢 And you? ★ 呢 and 尼(ní) have the same beginning sound n.	呢		
嗓	② sǎng　*n.* throat, voice 嗓子 throat, voice ★ 嗓 and 桑(sāng) differ only in tone.	嗓		
味	② wèi　*n.* taste; same sound as 为; similar to 妹 味道 taste, flavor, smell ★ 味 and 未(wèi, Lesson 28) have the same pronunciation.	味		
吸	② xī　*v.* breathe in, absorb same sound as 西；similar to 奶 呼吸 breath　　吸管 straw, sucker ★ 吸 and 及 have the same ending sound i.	吸		
响	(響) ① xiǎng　*n.* sound; *v.* ring; *adj.* noisy, loud 影响 influence　　音响 hi-fi　　响亮 loud and clear 交响乐 symphony ★ 响 and 向 differ only in tone.	响		
占	② zhàn　*v.* occupy, account for 占有 own, possess, occupy ★ Originally it meant fortune-telling.	占		
嘴	① zuǐ　*n.* mouth; similar to 止, 比 and 角 嘴巴 mouth ★ 嘴 and 觜(zī) have the same beginning sound z.	嘴		

课文中的其他生字

变	(變) ① biàn *v.* become, change；same sound as 便 变化 change 改(gǎi)变 change ★ Change with hand "又". 变(變) and 戀 have the same ending sound an.	变
例	① lì *n.* example; similar to 歹 例如 for example 例子 example 比例 proportion, scale ★ 例 and 列(liè) have the same beginning sound l.	例
影	① yǐng *n.* shadow 影子 shadow 电影 cinema, film 影响 infection, influence ★ The right part means shape or shadow. 影 and 景(jǐng) have the same ending sound ing.	影
注	① zhù *v.* pour 注意(yì) pay attention 注释 explanatory note ★ "氵" means water. 注 and 主 differ only in tone.	注

书写 WRITING

阝 阿 啊							啊
啊							

口 口 吗 喊 喊							喊
喊							

丿 勺 句

句　　　　　　　　　　　　　句

口 叩 叨 呢

呢　　　　　　　　　　　　　呢

亠 亣 亦 变

变　　　　　　　　　　　　　变

日 景 景 影 影

影　　　　　　　　　　　　　影

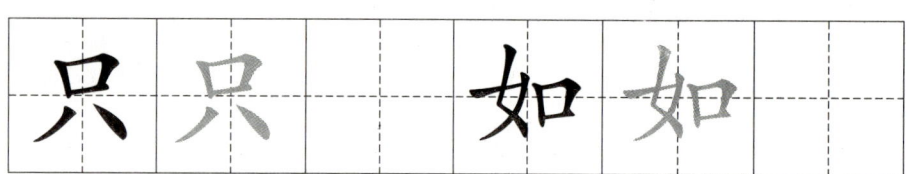

书写以前学过的字 Writing the characters you have learned before

只 只　　如 如

26

咱	咱		吵	吵	
古	古		品	品	
吓	吓		可	可	
奇	奇		吃	吃	
名	名		吐	吐	
吗	吗		器	器	
哪	哪		右	右	

骂	骂		听	听	
另	另		叫	叫	
命	命		知	知	
喝	喝		喜	喜	

第5课 目部 Eye ◎5

眼 睛

　　眼睛是心灵（líng）的窗户，用眼睛可以看到各种各样的东西，而别人也可以从你的眼睛里看到你心里的想法，你无法瞒过去。每天早上睡觉醒来，睁开眼睛，就开始看东西了。

　　有时候，看东西要睁大眼睛看，有时候却要眯着眼睛看。打（dǎ）枪的时候，一只眼闭（bì）着，一只眼眯着瞄准（zhǔn），盯着目标（biāo）看，心里盼望（wàng）着能打（dǎ）中（zhòng）。晚上开车的时候，要瞪大了眼睛，才能看清楚（qīng chu）前面路上的情况（qíng kuàng）。盲人的眼睛是瞎的，他们看不见，只能依靠（kào）和相信自己的耳朵。眉毛的作用是保护（hù）眼睛。

29

■ 部首 RADICAL 目 mù

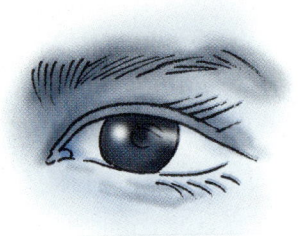

★ The character originally looked like an eye. Used as a radical, it is related to eyes, action of eyes, etc.

■ 生字 NEW CHARACTERS

课文中的目部字

瞪	③ dèng *v.* open one's eyes wide, stare at 瞪眼 stare ★ 瞪 and 登(dēng) differ only in tone.	瞪
盯	③ dīng *v.* gaze, stare at 盯人 run after, tail sb. ★ 盯 and 丁 have the same pronunciation.	盯
睛	① jīng *n.* eyeball; similar to 请; same sound as 京 眼睛 eye ★ 睛 and 青 have the same ending sound ing.	睛
瞒	(瞞) ③ mán *v.* hide the truth; similar to 两 ★ Don't let others to see the fact. 瞒 and 满 differ only in tone.	瞒
盲	③ máng *n.* blind; same sound as 忙 盲人 blind person ★ 盲 and 亡 have the same ending sound ang.	盲
眉	③ méi *n.* eyebrow; same sound as 没; similar to 尸 眉毛 brow ★ It looks like eyebrow over the eye.	眉

眯	③ mī *v.* narrow one's eyes ★ 眯 and 米 differ only in tone.	眯		
瞄	miáo *v.* take aim; similar to 田 瞄准(zhǔn) aim at, take aim ★ 瞄 and 苗(miáo) have the same pronunciation.	瞄		
盼	② pàn *v.* look, hope, expect; similar to 八 and 刀 盼望(wàng) expect, hope ★ 盼 and 分(fēn, Lesson 46) had similar sound in ancient times.	盼		
睡	① shuì *v.* sleep 睡觉 go to sleep ★ 睡 and 垂(chuí) have the same ending sound uei.	睡		
瞎	③ xiā *adj.* blind；*v.* be blind 瞎子 blind person ★ 瞎 and 害(hài) had similar sound in ancient times.	瞎		
眼	① yǎn *n.* eye; similar to 很 眼睛 eye ★ 眼 and 艮(gèn) had similar sound in ancient times.	眼		
睁	(睜) ② zhēng *v.* open the eyes ★ 睁 and 争 have the same pronunciation.	睁		

课文中的其他生字

| 靠 | ② kào   *v.* lean against, rely to, depend
依靠 depend on, rely on
★ 靠 and 告 have the same ending sound ɑo. | 靠 | | |
| 醒 | ② xǐng   *v.* wake; similar to 酒
★ The left part is wine. It originally meant waking up from a drunken stupor. 醒 and 星 differ only in tone. | 醒 | | |

|  | ② yī　*v.* lean against, depend on; same sound as 一
依靠 depend on, rely on
★ 依 and 衣 have the same pronunciation. | 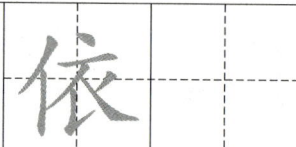 | | |

■ 生词 NEW WORDS

心灵 xīnlíng：heart, soul, spirit

打枪 dǎ qiāng：fire a rifle (or pistol)

打中 dǎzhòng：hit the mark

情况 qíngkuàng：situation, condition

■ 书写 WRITING

盯 盯 盯' 盯' 瞪 瞪						
瞪						

瞪

盯 盱 睛 瞒						
瞒						

瞒

⁊ ⁊ ⁊ 尸 眉						
眉						

眉

目′ 目″ 盯 盱 眰 晔 睡 睡

睡　　　　　　　睡

目 盯 晖 眸 瞎

瞎　　　　　　　瞎

西 酉 酉 酲 醒

醒　　　　　　　醒

第6课 页部 Head 🔍 6

■ 课文 TEXT

天气预报 (bào)

　　早上出门时，爸爸吩咐小林说："带上伞，天气预 (bào) 报说今天要下雨。"可小林看看天上没有云，认 (rèn) 为没问题，又觉得带雨伞麻烦，于是没带伞就上学去了。到了下午，一声雷响，顿时乌云一片，大雨来了。小林顾不得练习题也没做好，找了一顶帽 (mào) 子戴 (dài) 上，顶着一颗颗豆大的雨珠 (zhū) 回家去。头顶虽然没湿 (shī)，可是雨水顺着他的脖 (bó) 子流 (liú) 到领子里，他的衣服全湿 (quán shī) 了，成了落汤 (luò tāng) 鸡。可不到一顿饭 (fàn) 的工夫，小林的身上还没干，就雨过天晴了。小林对自己说："今天真不顺利 (lì)，看来还必须相信科学！"

部首 RADICAL 页（頁）yè

覺 覺 頁 頁 页

★ The character originally looked like a person with a big head. Used as a radical, it is related to head. It is usually written on the right.

生字 NEW CHARACTERS

课文中的页部字

顶	（頂）② dǐng *n.* top；*v.* carry on the head ★ Originally it meant the top of a head. 顶 and 丁 differ only in tone.	顶
顿	（頓）① dùn *n.* pause；*mw* [*measure word for meal*] 顿时 at once　停顿 pause　一顿饭 a meal ★ Originally it meant kowtow. 顿 and 屯 (tún) have the same ending sound uen.	顿
烦	（煩）① fán *adj.* be irritable 麻烦 bother, trouble　心烦 be perturbed ★ Originally it meant headache with fever.	烦
顾	（顧）① gù *v.* care for　回顾 look back　顾不得 can't take care of　照 (zhào) 顾 look after ★ Originally it meant turning around and looking at. 顾 (顧) and 雇(gù) have the same pronunciation.	顾
颗	（顆）② kē *mw* [*measure word for small things*] ★ Originally it meant small head, later it came to mean small round things. 颗 and 果 had similar sound in ancient times.	颗
领	（領）① lǐng *n.* neck, collar；*v.* lead 领子 collar　领带 necktie　领导 (dǎo) lead；leader ★ 领 and 令 differ only in tone.	领

顺	（顺）② shùn *adj.* fluent *v.* put in order 顺便 by the way 顺利(lì) smoothly, successfully, all right ★ Originally it meant to be obedient.	顺		
题	（题）① tí *n.* title 问题 problem, question 题目 title, exercise problem ★ Originally it meant forehead, later it came to mean title.	题		
须	（须）① xū *n.* beard; *v.* must 胡须 beard, moustache, whisker 必须 must, need ★ The left part is like beard.	须		
预	（预）① yù *adv.* beforehand; similar to 矛 预报(bào) forecast, predict ★ Originally it meant thinking before the things happen. 预 and 予(yǔ) differ only in tone.	预		

课文中的其他生字

豆	② dòu *n.* bean; same sound as 斗; similar to 立 豆腐 bean curd, tofu ★ The character originally looked like a bowl with base.	豆		
吩	② fēn 吩咐 tell, instruct ★ 吩 and 分 have the same pronunciation.	吩		
咐	② fù 吩咐 tell, instruct 嘱(zhǔ)咐 tell, instruct ★ 咐 and 付 have the same pronunciation.	咐		
夫	① fū *n.* husband, man; similar to 天 and 大 大夫 doctor 丈夫 husband 工夫 time ★ Originally it represented a male adult tying up his hair on the top of his head and fixing it with a hairpin.	夫		
科	① kē *n.* family of grain, section, branch of academic study 科学 science 文科 liberal arts ★ "禾" means grain.	科		

麻	① má *n.* pockmarks; *adj.* rough; similar to 广 and 林 麻烦 trouble, bother　麻醉 (zuì) anesthetize, hocus　大麻 hemp　★ The character originally looked like some hemp in the mountain.	麻		

 书写 WRITING

一　厂　屯　屯　顿

顿　　　　　　　　　顿

厂　厂　厄　顾

顾　　　　　　　　　顾

ㄱ　マ　マ　予　预

预　　　　　　　　　预

一　口　戸　豆　豆

豆　　　　　　　　　豆

一　二　夫　夫

夫　　　　　　　　　夫

肉（月）

■ 课文 TEXT

看医生

这两天，周老伯觉得身体不太舒服，于是就去看医

生。医生问他哪儿不舒服，周老伯抓抓（zhuā zhua）脑门，又摸摸（mō mo）胡

子，说："脖子、肩、背、腰、胳臂、腿、脚都不舒服。"

医生让（ràng）他脱下衣服，听了听胸口，看了看皮肤，又摸（mō）了

摸（mō）肚子，问："这几天肠胃好不好？"周老伯说："肠胃不

错，能吃很多，而且特别喜欢吃肥肉。"医生说："没病，

可能太累了，回去休息两天就没事了。还有，少吃肥

肉，太胖了对身体不好。"周老伯还不肯走，脸上很不

高兴，说："怎么不让我吃药（yào）？"医生说："你的身体没问

题，怎么能胡乱（luàn）吃药（yào）呢？"

部首 RADICAL 肉（月）ròu

口 夕 月 肉 肉

★ The character originally looked like a piece of meat cut in square shape. Because it was similar to "月(moon)", it was written in a wrong way when used as a radical which is often related to parts of the body. It is usually written as "月" on the left or at the bottom and called "ròuzìpáng". (Please see Lesson 18 "月".)

生字 NEW CHARACTERS

课文中的肉（月）部字

臂	③ bì, bei *n.* arm 胳臂 arm ★ 臂 and 辟 (bì) have the same pronunciation.	臂
脖	② bó *n.* neck；same sound as 伯 脖子 neck ★ 脖 and 孛 (bó) have the same pronunciation.	脖
肠	（腸）② cháng *n.* intestines；same sound as 常 肠子 intestines ★ 肠（腸）and 昜(yáng) have the same ending sound ɑng.	肠
肚	② dù *n.* abdomen, belly, stomach 肚子 abdomen, belly, stomach ★ 肚 and 土 have the same ending sound u.	肚
肥	② féi *adj.* fat, rich；similar to 把 and 吧 肥肉 fat, speck ★The right part originally looked like the joints on legs and arms, it meant so fat even on the joint.	肥
肤	（膚）② fū *n.* skin 皮肤 skin ★ 肤 and 夫 have the same pronunciation.	肤

胳	② gē　*n.* arm; same sound as 哥 胳臂 arm ★ 胳 and 各 differ only in tone.	胳		
胡	（鬍）② hú　*adv.* recklessly; similar to 姑 胡子 beard, moustache, whiskers　胡说 blether, wildly talk　★ Originally it meant the flesh chin. 胡 and 古 have the same ending sound u.	胡		
肩	② jiān　*n.* shoulder; similar to 尸 肩膀 (bǎng) shoulder ★ "户" looks like the part of body connecting arms with trunk of body.	肩		
脚	① jiǎo　*n.* feet same sound as 角; similar to 去 ★ 脚 and 却 (què) had similar sound in ancient times.	脚		
肯	② kěn　*v.* agree, be willing to similar to 齿 肯定 (dìng) affirm	肯		
脸	（臉）① liǎn　*n.* face ★ 脸 and 佥 (qiān) have the same ending sound ian.	脸		
脑	（腦）② nǎo　*n.* brain 脑门 forehead　大脑 brain　头脑 brain, head, mind 电脑 computer ★ The right part originally meant brain.	脑		
胖	② pàng　*adj.* fat ★ 胖 and 半 had similar sound in ancient times.	胖		
腿	① tuǐ　*n.* leg ★ 腿 and 退 (tuì, Lesson 14) differ only in tone.	腿		
脱	① tuō　*v.* take off; similar to 说 ★ Originally it meant losing weight, later on it meant "lose, take off". 脱 and 兑 (duì) had similar sound in ancient times.	脱		

胃	② wèi *n.* stomach; same sound as 为 and 位 胃口 appetite ★ The top part originally meant something in the stomach.	胃		
胸	(胷) ② xiōng *n.* chest ★ 胸 and 匈 (xiōng) have the same pronunciation.	胸		
腰	② yāo *n.* waist ★ 腰 and 要 differ only in tone.	腰		

课文中的其他生字

| 医 | (醫) ① yī *n.* medicine, doctor；*v.* cure
similar to 区；same sound as 一 and 衣

医生 doctor   医院 (yuàn) hospital | 医 | | |

生词 NEW WORDS

抓 zhuā：grasp

摸 mō：feel out, touch

书写 WRITING

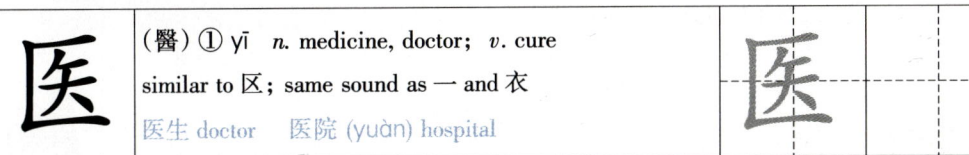

脖							

肋 肠 肠

肠　　　　　　　　　　　　　　　　　　　　　肠

月 肺 肺 肺

肺　　　　　　　　　　　　　　　　　　　　　肺

月 朏 脚 脚

脚　　　　　　　　　　　　　　　　　　　　　脚

月 脸 脸 脸

脸　　　　　　　　　　　　　　　　　　　　　脸

月 肝 胶 脑 脑

脑　　　　　　　　　　　　　　　　　　　　　脑

脬 脱 脱						
脱						

脱

肜 肋 肑 肑 胸 胸						
胸						

胸

一 厌 医						
医						

医

书写以前学过的字 Writing the characters you have learned before

有	有		能	能	
背	背		朋	朋	

■ 猜谜语 Riddles

脸上有，胃上有，背上胸上都有，腿上脚上也有；

头上无，身上无，耳上口上都无，手上指上也无。

(打一个字)

第8课 言部 Speech ⊚ 8

■ 课文 TEXT

爱^{ài}说话的小谢

小谢上课老爱^{ài}讲话，一会儿对左面的同学说他不认

识这个字，一会儿让右面的同学告诉他那个词是什么

意思^{yì sī}，有时又要和前面的同学讨论问题，有时还要与

后面的同学争论问题。老师批^{pī}评他说："小谢同学，请记

住：上课不应^{yīng}该随便讲话，尤其是老师在读课文的时

候。"小谢小声地说："谁随便讲话啦？我只是同他们谈

谈那些词语的意思^{yì sī}……"老师听到了很生气，警告他

说："老师说话还顶嘴，真是不可原谅。如果不改^{gǎi}正错

误，这次的考试成绩就扣十分。"

45

■ 部首 RADICAL 言（讠）yán

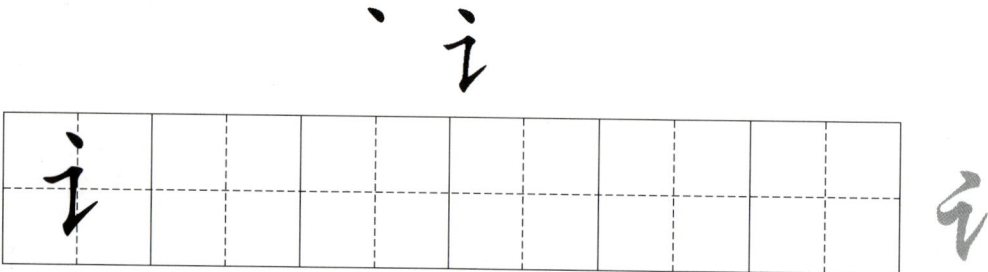

★ The original character had one stroke on top of "舌", meaning speaking with tongue. Used as a radical, it is related to language, speech, words, etc. When written on the left, it is changed to "讠".

■ 书写 WRITING

讠						

■ 生字 NEW CHARACTERS

课文中的言部字

词	（詞）① cí *n.* word；similar to 句 and 同 生词 new word 词典 dictionary ★ 词 and 司(sī) have the same ending sound -i.	词	
该	（該）① gāi *v.* ought to 应(yīng)该 should, must, ought ★ 该 and 亥(hài) have the same ending sound ai.	该	
话	（話）① huà *n.* saying, word same sound as 化；similar to 活 讲话 speak, talk 说话 speak ★ Speaking requires use of tongue.	话	
记	（記）① jì *v.* bear in mind, note, remember 忘记 forget 记得 remember 笔记 note 记者 journalist ★ 记 and 己 differ only in tone.	记	

46

讲	(講) ① jiǎng *v.* say；similar to 进 讲话 speak, talk 演(yǎn)讲 make a speech ★ 讲 and 井 have the same beginning sound j.	讲		
警	② jǐng *v.* alarm；similar to 句 警告 warn 警察(chá) policeman ★ 警 and 敬(jìng) differ only in tone.	警		
课	(課) ① kè *n.* class, lesson 上课 attend class 课文 text ★ 课 and 果 had similar sound in ancient times.	课		
谅	(諒) ① liàng *v.* forgive 原谅 forgive 谅解 understand ★ 谅 and 京 had similar sound in ancient times.	谅		
论	(論) ① lùn *v.* discuss；similar to 仑 争论 dispute, debate, argue 讨论 discuss ★ 论 and 仑(侖 lún) differ only in tone.	论		
评	(評) ① píng *v.* comment, judge 批(pī)评 criticize 评论 comment on ★ 评 and 平 have the same pronunciation.	评		
让	(讓) ① ràng *v.* allow, let 谦(qiān)让 modestly decline ★ 让 and 上 have the same ending sound ɑng.	让		
认	(認) ① rèn *v.* identify, recognize；same sound as 任 认识 know, understand 认为 consider, think 认真 earnest ★ 认 and 人 differ only in tone.	认		
识	(識) ① shí *v.* know；same sound as 十 and 时 认识 know, understand 知识 knowledge ★ 识 and 只 have the same ending sound -i.	识		
试	(試) ① shì *v.* examine, test, try similar to 成；same sound as 是 and 事 考试 exam ★ 试 and 式(shì) have the same pronunciation.	试		

谁	（誰）① shuí, shéi *pron.* who, whom similar to 住 ★ 谁 and 隹(zhuī) have the same ending sound uei.	谁		
诉	（訴）① sù　*v.* inform, tell; similar to 斥 告诉 tell ★ 诉 and 斥(chì) had similar sound in ancient times.	诉		
谈	（談）① tán　*v.* chat, talk; same sound as 痰 谈话 conversation ★ 谈 and 炎(yán) have the same ending sound an.	谈		
讨	（討）① tǎo　*v.* ask for, incur 讨论 discuss　讨厌(yàn) dislike ★ Originally it meant sending armed force to suppress.	讨		
误	（誤）① wù　*v.* hinder, miss; similar to 娱 错误 error, mistake　误会 mistake, misunderstand ★ 误 and 吴(wú) differ only in tone.	误		
谢	（謝）① xiè　*v.* thank; similar to 身 and 寸 感(gǎn)谢 thank ★ 谢 and 射(shè) had similar sound in ancient times.	谢		
语	（語）① yǔ　*n.* language; same sound as 雨 语言 language　汉语 Chinese　词语 words ★ 语 and 吾(wǔ) have similar ending sound ü and u.	语		

课文中的其他生字

| 绩 | （績）① jì　*n.* achievement

成绩 achievement, grade, result

★ 绩 and 责(zé) had similar sound in ancient times. | 绩 | | |
| 考 | ① kǎo　*v.* check; similar to 老

考试 exam, examination

★ Originally it meant long life. 考 and 丂 (kǎo) have the same pronunciation. | 考 | | |

| 师 | （師）① shī *n.* teacher, army

same sound as 尸

老师 teacher   师傅 master worker, mentor | 师 | | |
| 随 | （隨）② suí   *v.* adapt to, go with, follow

随便 casual, random, informal   随时 at any time | 随 | | |

■ 书写 WRITING

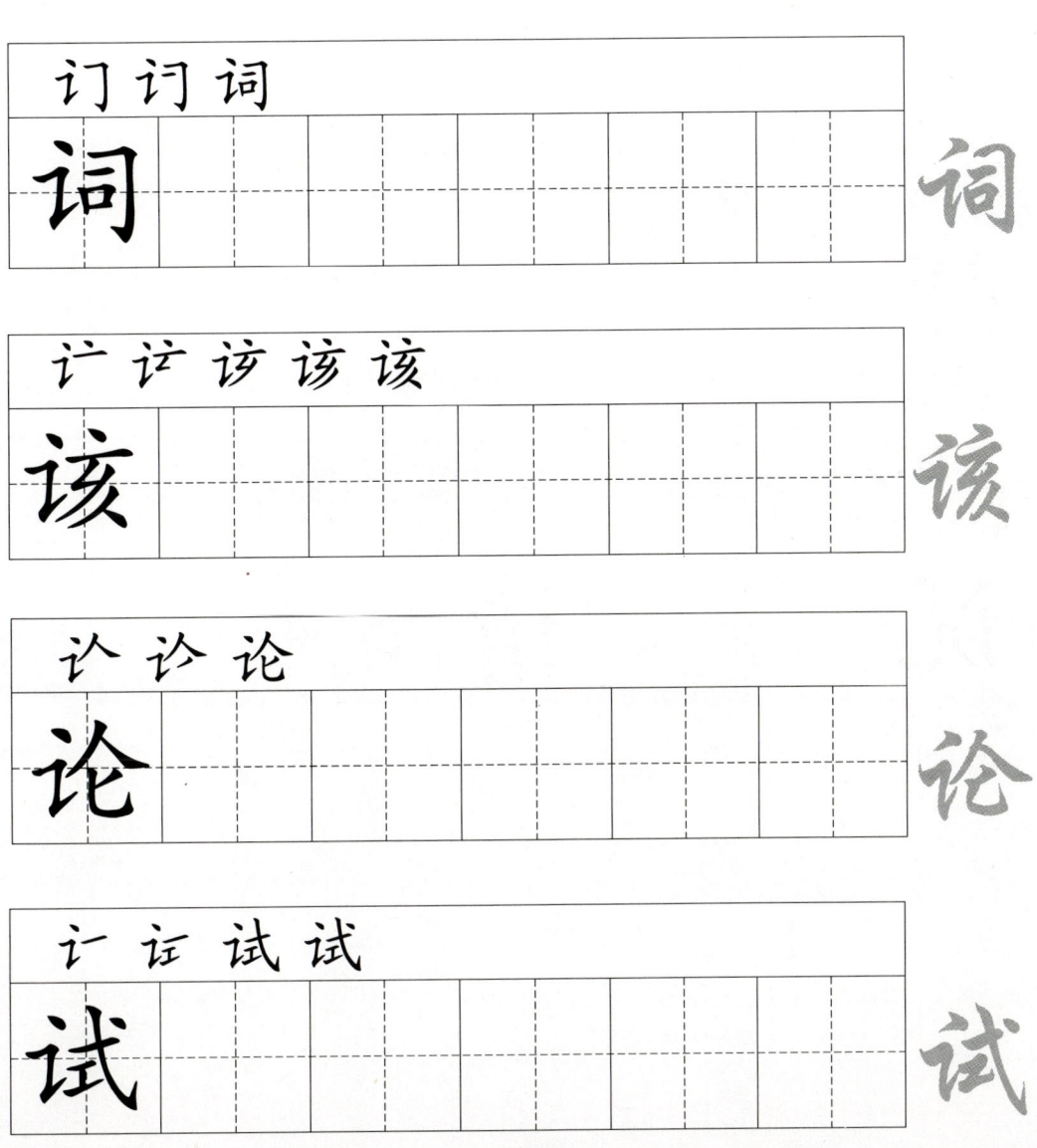

讠 计 计 诈 谁 谁

谁　　　　　　　　　　　　　　谁

屮 产 考

考　　　　　　　　　　　　　　考

丨 刂 厂 师

师　　　　　　　　　　　　　　师

书写以前学过的字 Writing the characters you have learned before

说 说 　 请 请

第9课 心部 Heart 🎧9

■ 课文 TEXT

一知半解

　　大卫已经习惯了中国的生活，心情一直很愉快。他不太懂中国话，但是很喜欢学。虽然常常会忘记，但慢慢地也学会了几句。他总是听人说"我去方便一下"，不知道是什么意思，就问一个中国朋友，别人告诉他说"方便"就是"上厕所"的意思。后来，有一次，他去看京剧表演，剧场休息的时候，他的一个朋友忽然诚恳地对他说："我想请您在方便的时候，一起合影留个纪念。您愿意吗？"大卫感到很吃惊，急忙说："我怎么会愿意呢？我在方便的时候从来不见人！"那个人知道大卫误会了，马上说："您别怕，我的意思是在您有空儿的时候。"

■ 部首　RADICAL　心（忄）xīn

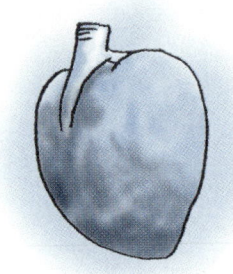 

★ The character originally looked like a heart. When used as a radical, it is related to heart, sensation, mood, thought, etc. When written on the left, it is changed to "忄" which is called "shùxīnpáng".

■ 书写　WRITING

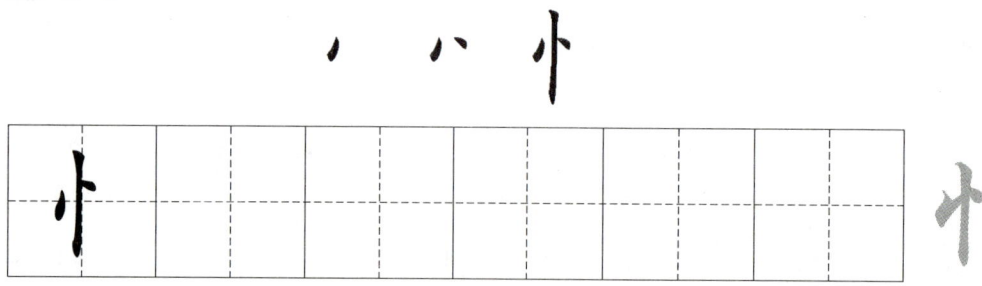

■ 生字　NEW CHARACTERS

课文中的心部字

懂	① dǒng　*v.* understand; similar to 重 懂得 understand ★ 懂 and 董 have the same pronunciation.	懂	
感	① gǎn　*v.* feel; similar to 喊 感觉 feel, sense　感谢 thank　感想 impressions ★ 感 and 咸(xián) have the same ending sound an.	感	
惯	(慣) ① guàn　*v.* indulge; similar to 母 and 贝 习惯 be used to, habituate ★ 惯 and 贯(guàn) have the same pronunciation.	惯	

忽	① hū *v.* ignore；*adv.* suddenly；same sound as 乎 and 呼 忽视 ignore, neglect 忽然 suddenly ★ 忽 and 勿 have the same ending sound u.	忽		
急	② jí *v.* worry；*adj.* urgent, anxious；similar to 争；same sound as 疾 急忙 haste, hurry 着急 feel anxious ★ The top part was changed from "及". 急 and 及 have the same pronunciation.	急		
惊	(驚) ② jīng *v.* shock, frighten 吃惊 have a fright, be surprised 惊奇 surprised, amazed ★ Originally it meant the startled horse. 惊 and 京 have the same pronunciation.	惊		
恳	② kěn *adj.* sincere；*v.* request 诚恳 sincere ★ 恳 and 艮(gèn) have the same ending sound en.	恳		
慢	① màn *adj.* slow ★ Originally it meant lazy, work slowly. 慢 and 曼(màn) have the same pronunciation.	慢		
念	① niàn *v.* miss, remember 留(liú)念 accept as a souvenir 想念 miss 纪(jì)念 memory ★ 念 and 今 had similar sound in ancient times.	念		
您	① nín *pron.* you ★ 您 and 你 have the same beginning sound n.	您		
怕	① pà *v.* fear, be afraid of；similar to 伯 害(hài)怕 be afraid, be scared 可怕 fearful, terrible ★ 怕 and 白 had similar sound in ancient times.	怕		
情	① qíng *n.* feeling, mood；same sound as 晴 心情 mood 爱(ài)情 love, affections 感情 sentiment ★ 情 and 青 differ only in tone.	情		
思	① sī *v.* consider, think；similar to 田 意思 meaning, idea 思想 thought 思考 consider ★ The top part meant brain in ancient times.	思		

息	① xī　*v.* breath, rest; same sound as 西　休息 rest, break, have a day off　★"自"originally meant nose. When you stop moving, the breathing through nose and the throbbing of heart will slow down.	息		
意	① yì　*n.* intention 注意 pay attention　意思 meaning, idea　主意 idea 意义 meaning ★ The top part is "音".	意		
愉	① yú　*adj.* happy 愉快 happy ★ 愉 and 俞(yú) have the same pronunciation.	愉		
愿	(願) ① yuàn　*v.* desire, hope, be willing 愿意 would like to, wish, be willing, want　　心愿 wish, dream　★ 愿 and 原 differ only in tone.	愿		
总	(總) ① zǒng　*adv.* after all, always 总是 always ★ 总 and 囪 have the same ending sound ong.	总		

课文中的其他生字

诚	(誠) ② chéng　*adj.* sincere, honest 诚恳 sincere　诚实 honest　诚心 sincere desire ★ 诚 and 成 have the same pronunciation.	诚		
剧	(劇) ② jù　*n.* drama; same sound as 句 and 俱 京剧 Beijing opera　剧场(chǎng) theater ★ 剧 and 居 differ only in tone.	剧		
演	① yǎn　*v.* act, perform 表演 act, perform　演员 actor, actress　演出 perform ★ 演 and 寅(yín) have similar pronunciation.	演		

■ 生词 NEW WORDS

厕所 cèsuǒ: W.C., lavatory

合影: take a group picture

书写 WRITING

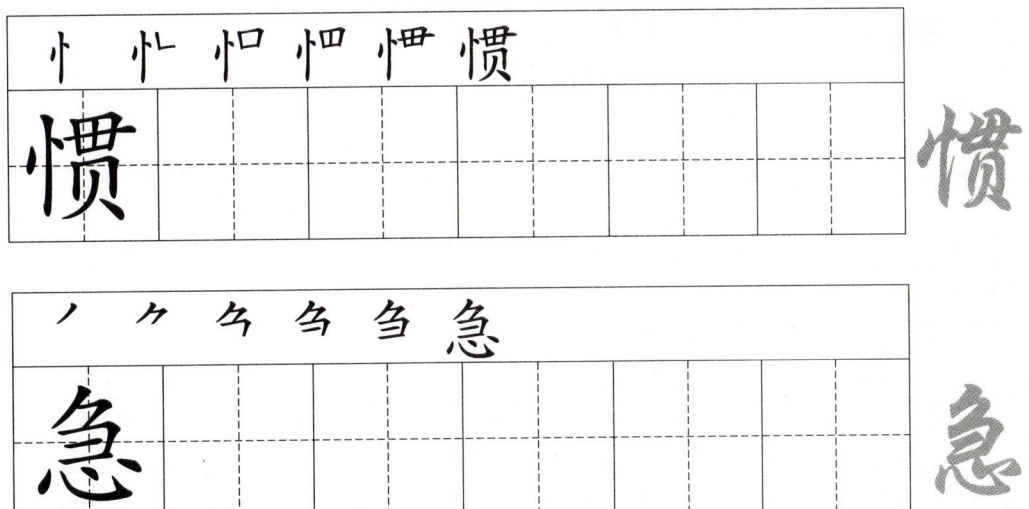

惯

急

书写以前学过的字 Writing the characters you have learned before

第10课 欠部 Yawn ● 10

■ 课文 TEXT

吹 牛

　　有个人很喜欢吹牛，他说他的歌唱得很好，是一个有名的歌手，到过欧（zhōu）洲的许多地方，那里的人都欢迎（yíng）他去唱歌。这次，他回到家乡，又向他的同乡吹起了牛，还说："我不会欺骗（piàn）你们的。"他的同乡说："你就把这里当做欧（zhōu）洲，唱一支歌给我们听听吧。"他同意了，于是来了许多人，都想听听他的歌声。他仰着脖子嚷起来："哎——嘿——呀——哩——哇——"等（děng）他唱完的时候，发觉差不多人都走光了，只有一个老头儿还在。那个人对老头儿说："也许只有你才是我的知音啊！"老头儿说："非常抱歉（bào）！您还是歇一会儿吧！您站着的这把椅（yǐ）子是我的，我等（děng）着拿回家呢。"

部首 RADICAL 欠 qiàn

良   夭   欠

★ The chara cter originally looked like a person yawning with his mouth open. Used as a radical, it is related to activities involving an open mouth, and usually written on the right. It is also used as sound part of characters with the pronunciation "an".

生字 NEW CHARACTERS

课文中的欠部字

吹	① chuī *v.* blow, boast similar to 欢 吹牛 talk big	吹
次	① cì *n.* order, sequence；*adj.* second, next 这次 this time	次
歌	① gē *n.* song 唱歌 sing ★ 歌 and 哥 have the same pronunciation.	歌
欧	(歐) ③ ōu 欧洲(zhōu) Europe ★欧 and 区 (used as a family name, pronounced as Ōu) have the same pronunciation.	欧
欺	② qī *v.* deceive, bully；same sound as 七 欺骗(piàn) deceive, cheat 欺侮(wǔ) bully ★ 欺 and 其 differ only in tone.	欺
歉	② qiàn *v.* be apologetic；similar to 并 抱(bào)歉 sorry ★ 歉 and 兼(jiān) have the same ending sound ian.	歉

| 歇 | ② xiē　v. have a rest；similar to 喝
歇一会儿 rest for a while
★ 歇 and 曷(hé) had similar sound in ancient times. | 歇 | | |

课文中的其他生字

哎	② āi　int. [particle indicating mood] ★ 哎 and 艾 differ only in tone.	哎		
嘿	② hēi　int. [particle indicating mood] ★ 嘿 and 黑 have the same pronunciation.	嘿		
哩	② li [particle indicating mood] ★ 哩 and 里 differ only in tone.	哩		
嚷	② rǎng　v. shout ★ 嚷 and 襄 (xiāng) have the same ending sound ang.	嚷		
哇	② wā　onomatopoeia [particle indicating mood] ★ 哇 and 圭(guī) had similar sound in ancient times.	哇		
许	(許) ① xǔ　v. promise, allow 许多 many, much　不许 disallow　也许 maybe ★ "讠" means speech. 许 and 午 have similar ending sound ü and u.	许		
呀	① yā　int. [particle indicating mood] ★ 呀 and 牙 differ only in tone.	呀		
仰	② yǎng　v. face upward, rely on ★ 仰 and 卬(áng) have the same ending sound ang.	仰		

站	① zhàn *v.* stand, stop; *n.* stop 站起来 stand up 车站 bus stop 火车站 train station ★ "立" means stand or stop. 站 and 占 have the same pronunciation.	站		
支	① zhī *n.* branch; *v.* raise, support, pay; *mw* [*measure word for music*] 支持(chí) support 支付 pay 一支歌 a song ★ Originally it meant a hand holding a branch. "又" looked like a hand.	支		

生词 NEW WORDS

光：all gone; smooth

知音：bosom friend

书写 WRITING

冫	冫	次					
次							

次

一	丁	又	区	欧			
欧							

欧

丷	丷	屴	当	当	尃	兼	兼	兼	歉
歉									

歉

日 号 昻 昌 歇

歇　　　　　　　　　歇

宀 吥 喡 嘾 嚷 嚷 嚷 嚷 嚷

嚷　　　　　　　　　嚷

亻 仁 仰 仰

仰　　　　　　　　　仰

立 꾸 站 站

站　　　　　　　　　站

一 十 支

支　　　　　　　　　支

书写以前学过的字 Writing the characters you have learned before

欢 欢

第11课 手部 Hand 🔘 11

■ 课文 TEXT

^{qǐ}
一起干

为了保持卫生、预防和抵抗疾病、保护大家的健

康，同学们要搞一次大扫除。小王是班长，他指挥大家

一起干。他先拉开窗帘、推开门，抱起垃圾桶，把它搬

到外面，接着就抓起扫把扫地；小牛提着水，小马抢着

拿起拖把就拖地板；小金找来一条毛巾，擦起了黑板；

小丁把掉在地上的书捡起来，把一排排的桌子和椅子都

摆整齐。最后，小王张开手掌到处摸了摸，向大家招了

招手，说："今天教室打扫得挺干净的，大家都应该得

到表扬。"

■ 部首 RADICAL 手（扌）shǒu

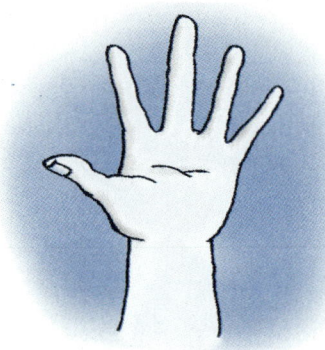

★ The character originally looked like a hand with five fingers. Used as a radical, it is related to hand, action of hands, etc. When written on the left, it is changed to "扌", and called "tíshǒupáng". It has the same meaning with "又", "寸", "爪", "夊" and "廾".

■ 书写 WRITING

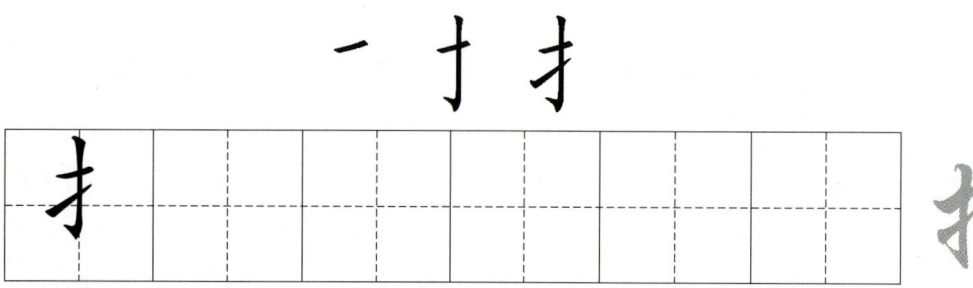

扌								扌

■ 生字 NEW CHARACTERS

课文中的手部字

摆	（擺）① bǎi v. put, place, sway similar as 四 and 去 ★ 摆 and 罢(bà) have the same beginning sound b.	摆	
搬	① bān v. take away, move ★ 搬 and 般(bān) have the same pronunciation.	搬	
抱	① bào v. hold (or carry) in the arm, hug 抱歉(qiàn) be sorry, regret ★ 抱 and 包(bāo) differ only in tone.	抱	

擦	① cā *v.* rub, wipe ★ 擦 and 察(chá) have the same ending sound a.	擦		
持	① chí *v.* hold, grasp；similar to 土 and 寸 保持 maintain, keep 坚(jiān)持 persist in, insist on ★ 持 and 寺 (sì) have the same ending sound -i.	持		
打	① dǎ *v.* beat, hit, do, play 打球 play ball 打电话 make a phone call 打的 take a taxi 打扫 clean ★ 打 and 丁 have the same beginning sound d.	打		
抵	③ dǐ *v.* resist；similar to 低 and 婚 抵抗 fight against ★ 抵 and 氏(dǐ) have the same pronunciation.	抵		
掉	① diào *v.* drop, fall, lose similar to 早 ★ 掉 and 卓(zhuó) had similar sound in ancient times.	掉		
搞	① gǎo *v.* do ★ 搞 and 高 differ only in tone.	搞		
护	(護) ② hù *v.* protect 保护 protect 护士 nurse 护照(zhào) passport ★ 护 and 户 have the same pronunciation.	护		
挥	(揮) ② huī *v.* brandish, command；same sound as 灰 指挥 command, direct ★ The right part is "军" which means army. It means commanding an army.	挥		
捡	(撿) ② jiǎn *v.* pick up similar to 脸 and 险 ★ 捡 and 佥(qiān) have the same ending sound ian.	捡		
接	① jiē *v.* catch, connect, receive；similar to 立 and 女 接着 catch, go on with ★ 接 and 妾(qiè) have the same ending sound ie.	接		

抗	② kàng　*v.* combat, fight 抵抗 resist, stand up to ★ 抗 and 亢(kàng) have the same pronunciation.	抗		
拉	① lā　*v.* pull similar to 位 ★ 拉 and 立 have the same beginning sound l.	拉		
摸	② mō　*v.* feel out, touch similar to 日 and 大 ★ 摸 and 莫(mò) differ only in tone.	摸		
排	① pái　*v.* arrange；*n.* row, line 安(ān)排 arrange, plan ★ 排 and 非 had similar sound in ancient times.	排		
抢	(搶) ② qiǎng　*v.* rob, snatch ★ 抢 and 仓（倉）have the same ending sound ang.	抢		
扫	(掃) ② sǎo　*v.* clear away, sweep；similar to 妇 扫(sào)把 broom　　打扫 clean ★ Originally the right part was "帚", meaning the broom.	扫		
提	① tí　*v.* bring up, carry, lift；same sound as 题 提高 advance, improve　　提供 offer, provide ★ 提 and 是 had similar sound in ancient times.	提		
挺	① tǐng　*adj.* straight, erect；*v.* stick out 挺好 good, nice ★ 挺 and 廷(tíng) differ only in tone.	挺		
推	① tuī　*v.* push；similar to 谁 推拿 massage (a kind of Chinese traditional medical treatment) ★ 推 and 隹(zhuī) have the same ending sound uei.	推		
拖	② tuō　*v.* pull, drag same sound as 脱 拖把 mop	拖		

扬	（揚）① yáng *v.* raise；similar to 肠；same sound as 羊 表扬 praise, commend ★ 扬（揚）and 易 (yáng) have the same sound.	扬		
掌	① zhǎng *n.* palm；similar to 常 鼓(gǔ)掌 clap one's hands, applause 掌握(wò) grasp, master 手掌 palm ★ 掌 and 尚(shàng) have the same ending sound ang.	掌		
招	② zhāo *v.* wave, call；similar to 绍 打招呼 greet sb. ★ 招 and 召(zhào) differ only in tone.	招		
找	① zhǎo *v.* look for, seek similar to 我 找人 look for sb. 找钱 give change	找		
指	① zhǐ *n.* finger；*v.* point 指挥 command 指引 direct, guide ★ 指 and 旨(zhǐ) have the same pronunciation.	指		
抓	② zhuā *v.* grasp ★ 抓 and 爪 differ only in tone.	抓		

■ 生词 NEW WORDS

预防 yùfáng：prevent, defend, guard against

大扫除 dàsǎochú：give a thorough cleaning

班长 bānzhǎng：class monitor, squad leader

窗帘 chuānglián：curtain

板 bǎn：board [地板 floorboard, floor   黑板 blackboard]

起 qǐ：rise, start

整齐 zhěngqí：tidy, orderly

■ 书写 WRITING

扌 抵抵

抵

扌 扌 扩 捵 捵 掉

掉

扌 扌 扩 挥

挥

扩 拾 捡 捡

捡

扩 扩 扩 抗

抗

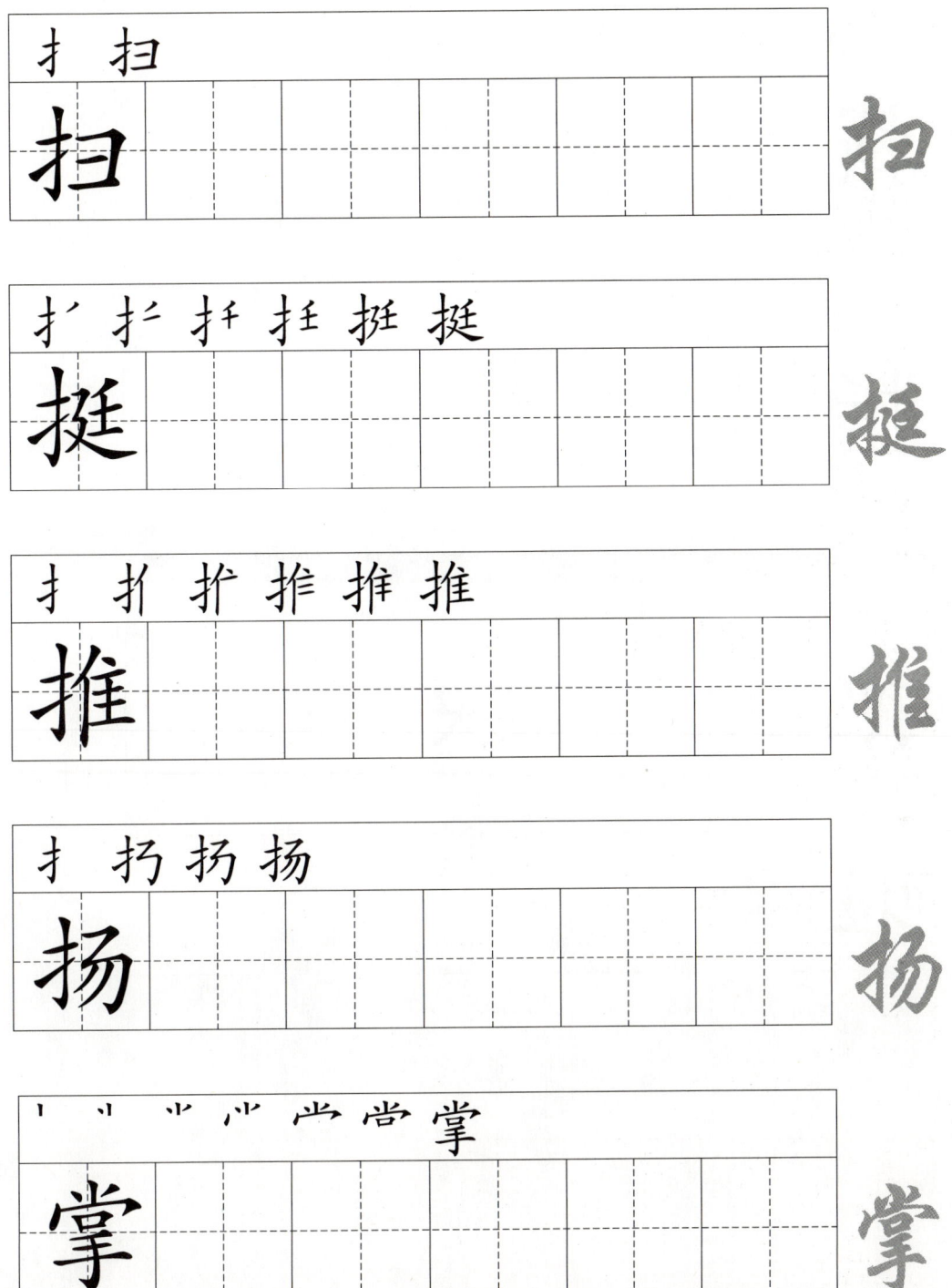

扫

挺

推

扬

掌

扌 扌 找 找 找

找　　　　　　　　　　找

扌 扌 扩 指

指　　　　　　　　　　指

书写以前学过的字 Writing the characters you have learned before

把 把　　换 换

啦 啦

第12课 攵部 Action with Hand  12

■ 课文 TEXT

妙 语

有这么一个故事：一位外国数学家到中国来访问，

政府官员整齐地排成一排，向他致敬，和他握手、照相
^{fǔ} ^{zhào}

并欢送他。他感动地说：你们太客气了，我真是不敢当。
^{sòng} ^{dòng}

这次来访问，参观了很多地方，收获很多，使我对你们
^{huò}

的看法有了很大的改变，你们的数学教育很有成效。我

会设计一个新的项目，今后我们可以放心地合作了。不

过，我还有一个问题要向你们请教：你们的语言太奇妙

了，为什么"救火"和"救命"都用"救"？命应该救，
^{yīng}

火是应该灭的呀！还有，"一会儿"和"不一会儿"的意
^{yīng} ^{miè}

思是一样的；"我方大胜敌人"和"我方大败敌人"的意

思也一样，胜利好像总是属于你们。这样的例子数也数
^{shǔ}

不过来。

■ 部首 RADICAL　攵 pū

★ The character originally looked like a hand holding a stick. Used as a radical, it is related to hand, action of hands, hit, etc. and written on the right, called "fǎnwénpáng". It has the same meaning as "手", "又", "寸", "殳", etc.

■ 书写 WRITING

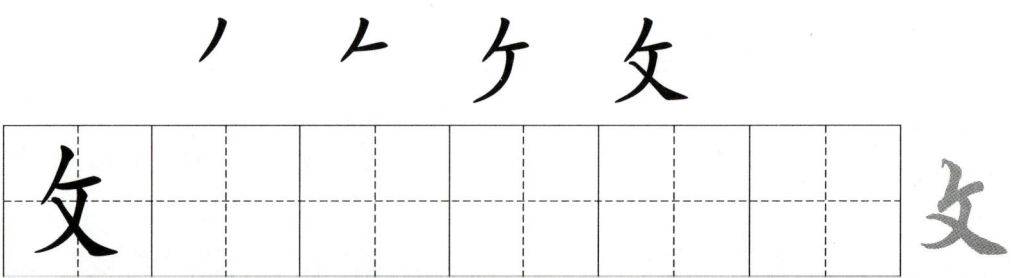

攵							攵

■ 生字 NEW CHARACTERS

课文中的攵部字

败	（敗）② bài　v. defeat, fail 失败 be defeated ★ 败 and 贝 have the same beginning sound b.	败	
敌	（敵）② dí　v. resist, oppose;　n. enemy similar to 舌 敌人 enemy	敌	
放	① fàng　v. put 放心 set one's mind at rest ★ 放 and 方 differ only in tone.	放	

改	① gǎi *v.* change; similar to 记 改变 change ★ 改 and 己 had similar sound in ancient times.	改		
敢	① gǎn *v.* dare similar to 耳 and 工; same sound as 感 不敢当 don't deserve this	敢		
故	① gù *adj.* former; similar to 姑 and 胡 故事 story ★ 故 and 古 differ only in tone.	故		
教	① jiào *v.* let *n.* education, religion; jiāo *v.* teach similar to 老 and 子; same sound as 叫 教育 education　教室 classroom　★ 教 and 孝(xiào) have the same ending sound iao.	教		
敬	② jìng *v.* respect 敬礼(lǐ) salute　致敬 salute, pay a tribute to 尊(zūn)敬 respect	敬		
救	② jiù *v.* rescue, save, halp 救命 help ★ 救 and 求 have the same ending sound iou.	救		
收	① shōu *v.* receive, get; similar to 叫 收到 have got, receive ★ 收 and 丩(jiū) have the same ending sound ou.	收		
数	(數) ① shù *n.* number; shǔ *v.* count similar to 米 and 女　数学 mathematics ★ 数 and 娄(lóu) had similar sound in ancient times.	数		
效	② xiào *v.* imitate, devote; similar to 校 and 较 效果 effect ★ 效 and 交 have the same ending sound iao.	效		
整	① zhěng *v.* put in order; *adj.* whole; similar to 束 整齐 in order　整理 clean up, tidy up ★ 整 and 正 differ only in tone.	整		

| 政 | ① zhèng　*n.* politics
政府(fǔ) government　政治(zhì) politics
★ 政 and 正 have the same pronunciation. | 政 | | |
| 致 | ② zhì　*v.* send, deliver, result in
致敬(jìng) salute, pay a tribute to
★ 致 and 至 have the same pronunciation. | 致 | | |

课文中的其他生字

访	(訪) ① fǎng　*v.* call on, visit; similar to 放 访问 visit ★ The left part means speech. 访 and 方 differ only in tone.	访		
观	(觀) ① guān　*v.* look at, watch; same sound as 关 参观 visit ★ "见" means seeing. 观（觀）and 鹳(guàn) differ only in tone.	观		
计	(計) ① jì　*v.* count, calculate; *n.* idea, plan same sound as 记　设计 design　计划(huà) plan 计算(suàn)机 computer ★ "言" and "十" together mean to calculate.	计		
设	(設) ① shè　*v.* set up, establish, found 设计 design, plan　设想 imagine, conceive	设		
胜	(勝) ① shèng　*v.* defeat, win, success 胜利(lì) victory ★ Originally "力" meant force, and "朕 (zhèn)" indicates the sound. Now 胜 and 生 differ only in tone.	胜		
示	① shì　*v.* show, notify, instruct 表示 express, show　出示 show ★ This is a radical which is usually related to religion.	示		
握	① wò　*v.* grasp, hold 握手 shake hands　掌握 master, hold ★握 and 屋 have the same beginning sound u.	握		

| 项 | (项) ① xiàng　*n.* nape, sum, term

same sound as 向 and 象　　项目 item

★ 项 and 工 had similar sound in ancient times. | 项 | |
| 育 | ① yù　*v.* give birth to; similar to 胃
教育 schooling, education
★ Originally the top part is the inverted "子". It meant giving birth to a baby. | 育 | |

■ 生词 NEW WORDS

官员 guānyuán：officer, official

欢送 huānsòng：send off

感动 gǎndòng：affect, touch, move

灭 miè：destroy

属于 shǔyú：belong to

■ 书写 WRITING

| フ フ 孑 改 | | | | | | | 改 |
| 改 | | | | | | | |

| フ コ 干 开 开 耳 耳 敢 | | | | | | | 敢 |
| 敢 | | | | | | | |

一 ⺿ 芍 苟 敬

敬　　　　　　　　　敬

乚 丩 收

收　　　　　　　　　收

一 二 亍 汞 示

示　　　　　　　　　示

丶 亠 云 去 育

育　　　　　　　　　育

书写以前学过的字 Writing the characters you have learned before

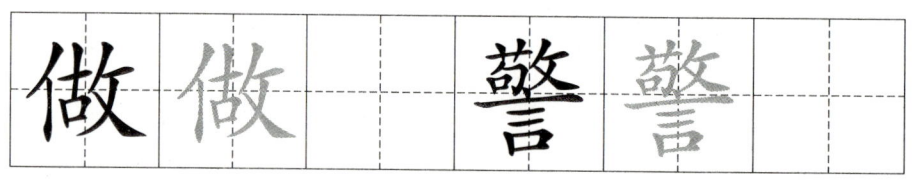

做　做　　　警　警

课文 TEXT

按上面写的做

　　从前，有一户人家住在离马路没几步远的房子里，到了晚上，有些过路人经常在他家的房子旁边小便。于是，这家主人就在那里放了一块警告牌，上面写道："过路人等，不得在此地小便！"开始几天，这块牌子还是很有用处的，没有人在那里小便了；可又过了几天，虽然牌子还插在那里，但还是有人到那里小便。这家主人非常愤怒。有一次，他找到机会，快步走上前，一把抓住一个正在那里"方便"的人，指着牌子，咬牙切齿地骂道："你瞎了眼吗？没看见上面的字吗？你不觉得可耻吗？"那人歪着头，用很肯定的语调说："请别动武！我就是按上面写的做的。"主人抬头一看，那句话变成了："过路人，等不得，在此地小便！"

75

■ 部首 RADICAL　止 zhǐ

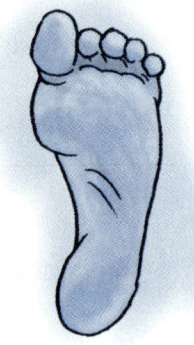

★ The character originally looked like a foot with three toes. Used as a radical, it is related to feet, action of feet, etc. and has the same meaning as "足", "走", "辶", "彳", "疋", "夂", etc. It is also used as a sound part of characters with the pronunciation zhi or chi.

■ 生字 NEW CHARACTERS

课文中的止部字

耻	④ chǐ　*v.* feel shamed; same sound as 尺 and 齿 可耻 shameful ★ 耻 and 止 have the same ending sound -i.	耻		
此	② cǐ　*pron.* this; similar to 比, 化 and 嘴 ★ The right part was changed from "人". It means the place where a person is standing. 此 and 止 have the same ending sound -i.	此		
歪	② wāi　*adj.* askew, slanting; *v.* recline ★ "不" and "正" mean not straight.	歪		
武	② wǔ　*n.* military strength, force; same sound as 五 and 午; similar to 试　动武 use force　武力 force, armed might　★ "戈" looks like a weapon. It means holding a weapon and fighting.	武		

课文中的其他生字

按	② àn *v.* press, control 按照(zhào) according to ★The left part is "手". 按 and 安(ān, Lesson 41) differ only in tone.	按		
插	② chā *v.* insert, stick into 插头 plug 插座 socket, outlet ★ 插 and 臿(chā) have the same pronunciation.	插		
调	① diào *v.* transfer, move；*n.* tone tiáo *v.* mix, adjust 语调(diào) intonation 空调(kōngtiáo) air conditioner	调		
愤	② fèn *n.* anger 愤怒 be angry ★ 愤 and 贲(bēn) have the same ending sound en.	愤		
怒	② nù *v.* get angry 发怒 be angry at ★ 怒 and 奴(nú) differ only in tone.	怒		
牌	② pái *n.* board, plate, brand, cards 牌子 billboard, brand 名牌 famous brand 打牌 play cards ★ "片" means a slice piece of wood. 牌 and 卑 (bēi) had similar sound in ancient times.	牌		
抬	① tái *v.* raise, uplift; similar to 始 ★ The left part is "手". 抬 and 台 (tái, Lesson 24) have the same pronunciation.	抬		
咬	② yǎo *v.* bite; similar to 校 and 较 咬牙切(qiè)齿 gnash one's teeth at ★ The left part is "口". 咬 and 交 have the same ending sound iao.	咬		

■ 生词 NEW WORDS

马路 mǎlù：street, road

过路 guòlù：pass by

■ 书写　WRITING

止	止	此							
此									

此

一	二	正	武	武					
武									

武

扌	扌	扦	扦	抔	抔	插	插	插	
插									

插

忄	忄	忄	忄	愤	愤				
愤									

愤

片	片	牌	牌	牌	牌				
牌									

牌

扌 扚 抬

| 抬 | | | | | | | |

抬

书写以前学过的字Writing the characters you have learned before

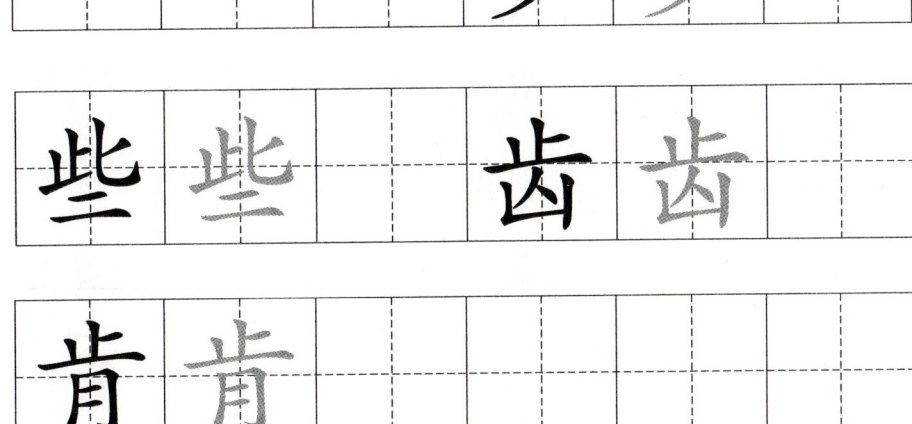

第14课 辶部 Walk & Road 🔘 14

课文 TEXT

运 气

　　一天夜里，马先生梦见自己正在逛街，半道上遇见一个老同学，他邀请道："欢迎到我新建造的房子来做客！"正在这时，一个小偷进了他家。当小偷走进院子时，远远地听到马先生在说话，以为他还没睡，就躲避在一旁，不敢进房间。过了一会儿，小偷走近了些，在通过窗户边时，又听到马先生说："请进吧！"小偷认为马先生已经发觉他还在院子里，于是就马上退了出去。这时，又听到马先生说："不送，不送。"小偷怕马先生追

出来，被逼得没办法了，就迅速往回跑，连头也不敢回。

他一边逃一边想：我今天运气真好，如果走得迟了，还

不知道会怎么样呢！

部首 RADICAL 辶 chuò

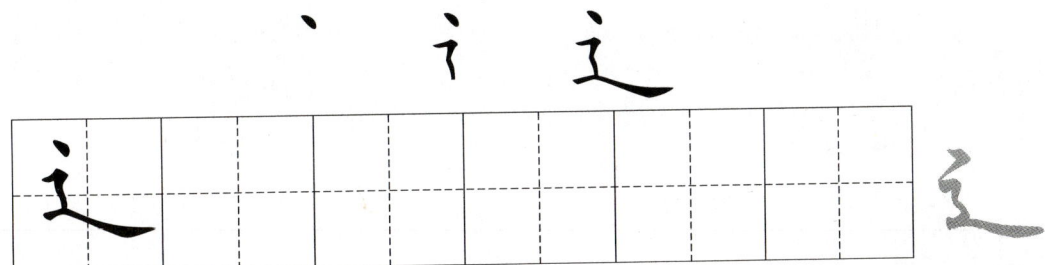

★ The character originally was composed of "行" and "止" and looked like feet walking on a road. Used as a radical, it is related to road, feet, action of feet, etc. It is usually written at the bottom and called "zǒuzhǐdǐ". It has the same meaning as "止", "足", "走", "彳", "疋", "夂", etc.

书写 WRITING

丶   冫   辶

辶   辶

生字 NEW CHARACTERS

课文中的辶部字

逼	② bī *v.* force, compel 逼真 lifelike, clear ★ 逼 and 畐(bī) have the same pronunciation.	逼
避	② bì *v.* avoid, prevent; same sound as 币 躲避 hide (oneself), dodge 避免(miǎn) avoid, avert ★ 避 and 辟(bì) have the same pronunciation.	避
迟	(遲) ① chí *adj.* late; same sound as 持 迟到 be late ★ 迟 and 尺 differ only in tone.	迟

逛	② guàng　*v.* stroll, ramble 逛街 take a walk on the street 逛商店(diàn) window-shopping ★ 逛 and 狂(kuáng) have the same ending sound uang.	逛		
近	① jìn　*adj.* near, close；similar to 听；same sound as 进 最近 recently ★ 近 and 斤 differ only in tone.	近		
连	(連) ① lián　*v.* connect, link ★ Inside is "车". Originally it meant to connect war chariots during the war in ancient times.	连		
送	① sòng　*v.* send off, give, deliver similar to 关 欢送 send off　送礼 give sb. a gift　送信 deliver a letter	送		
速	② sù　*adj.* fast, rapid；*v.* invite 迅速 fast, quick　速度(dù) speed ★ Originally it meant invitation. 速 and 束 have the same ending sound u.	速		
逃	② táo　*v.* escape, flee 逃走 escape, flee ★ 逃 and 兆(zhào) have the same ending sound ao.	逃		
通	① tōng　*v.* go to, lead to；similar to 痛 and 甬 通过 pass, cross　通知 notify, inform ★ 通 and 甬(yǒng) have the same ending sound ong.	通		
退	① tuì　*v.* move back similar to 腿 退后 move back　退步 lag behind	退		
迅	② xùn　*adj.* fast 迅速 fast, quick ★ Originally it meant "run fast". 迅 and 讯 (xùn) have the same pronunciation.	迅		
邀	② yāo　*v.* invite；same sound as 腰 邀请 invite, request ★ 邀 and 敫(jiǎo) have the same ending sound iao.	邀		

迎	① yíng *v.* meet, greet; similar to 仰 欢迎 welcome ★ 迎 and 卬(áng) had similar sound in ancient times.	迎		
遇	① yù *v.* meet; similar to 离; same sound as 预 遇到 meet with, run into ★ Originally it meant to meet sb. or sth. on the way. 遇 and 禺(yú) differ only in tone.	遇		
远	(遠) ① yuǎn *adj.* far away ★ 远 and 元 differ only in tone.	远		
运	(運) ① yùn *v.* carry; similar to 远 运气 fortune, luck 运动(dòng) sports, movement ★ 运 and 云 differ only in tone.	运		
造	② zào *v.* build, make, arrive at 建造 build 制(zhì)造 make ★ Originally it meant "visit". 造 and 告 have the same ending sound ɑo.	造		
追	② zhuī *v.* chase ★ 追 and 𠂤(duī) have the same ending sound uei.	追		

课文中的其他生字

躲	② duǒ *v.* avoid, hide 躲避 avoid, hide ★ "身" means body. 躲 and 朵 have the same pronunciation.	躲		
梦	(夢) ② mèng *n.*, *v.* dream 做梦 dream 梦见 / 梦到 dream of sth./sb.	梦		
偷	② tōu *v.* steal 小偷 thief, pickpocker ★ The left part is "人". 偷 and 俞(yú) had similar sound in ancient times.	偷		

| 往 | ① wǎng　*v.* go；*prep.* toward

similar to 住；same sound as 网 | | 往 | | |

■ 书写 WRITING

丿 刂 刂 刂 兆 兆 兆 逃

逃　　　　　　　　　　　　　逃

フ フ 甬 通

通　　　　　　　　　　　　　通

飞 飞 汛 迅

迅　　　　　　　　　　　　　迅

丶 丨 匚 卬 迎

迎　　　　　　　　　　　　　迎

冂 日 禺 禺 禺 遇

遇　　　　　　　　　　　　　遇

84

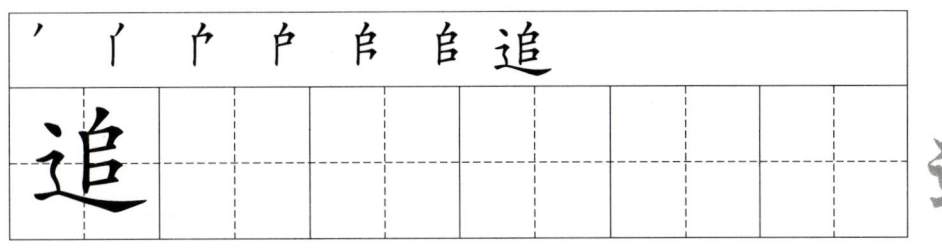

书写以前学过的字 Writing the characters you have learned before

还	还		这	这	
过	过		边	边	
进	进		道	道	
腿	腿		随	随	

第15课 走部 Walk 🔵 15

■ 课文 TEXT

不睡懒觉

　　小赵每天早上都喜欢睡懒觉。这天，他一觉醒来，发现时间已经来不及了，赶快起来穿衣服，生怕上课迟到。他拿出一套西装，可是，慌慌张张，他越是想快，就越是套不上，他急得不得了，这才发现原来把衣服穿反了。时间越来越少，他连饭也顾不上吃就出门了。在路中央，他拦下一辆出租车，让司机拼命地开快车，想赶上前面所有的车子。但有趣的是，这车子好像就是跟在别人后面跑不快，越想超就越是超不过。小赵越急，车子越慢。小赵急得大叫一声"啊！"还好，原来是一个梦。小赵看看时间还早，心想：这个梦真可怕，真应该趁早改掉这个坏毛病。想着想着，又睡着了。

86

部首 RADICAL 走 zǒu

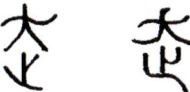

★ The character originally was composed of "夭" (like swinging one's arms while running) and "止". Used as a radical, it is related to running, action of feet, etc. It is usually written at the bottom and called "zǒuzìdǐ". It has the same meaning as "辶", "止", "足", "彳", "疋", "夂", etc.

生字 NEW CHARACTERS

课文中的走部字

超	② chāo *v.* exceed; similar to 招 and 绍 超过 overrun, exceed 超市 supermarket ★ 超 and 召 have the same ending sound ao.	超
趁	② chèn *conj.* while 趁早 as early as possible ★ 趁 and 诊(zhěn) have the same ending sound en.	趁
赶	(趕) ② gǎn *v.* catch up with; same sound as 感 and 敢 赶快 hurry ★ 赶 and 干 differ only in tone.	赶
起	① qǐ *v.* rise, get up; similar to 记 起床 get up 一起 together, in all ★ 起 and 己 have the same ending sound i.	起
趣	② qù *n.* interest; similar to 取; same sound as 去 有趣 interesting, amusing 兴趣 interest ★ 趣 and 取 differ only in tone.	趣

| 越 | ② yuè　*v.* get over, exceed；similar to 成
越来越 more and more　越···越··· the more... the more...
★ 越 and 戉(yuè) have the same pronunciation. | 越 | | |
| 赵 | （趙）③ Zhào　*n.* family name
赵小姐 Miss Zhao
★ Originally it was written as "趙", having the same ending sound ɑo as "肖(Xiāo)". | 赵 | | |

课文中的其他生字

慌	② huāng　*adj.* flurried；similar to 忘 慌张 flurry ★ The left part is "忄". 慌 and 荒(huāng) have the same pronunciation.	慌		
拦	（攔）② lán　*v.* bar, block ★ The left part is "手". 拦 and 兰 (lán) have the same pronunciation.	拦		
懒	（懶）② lǎn　*adj.* lazy；similar to 束 and 贝 睡懒觉 sleep late, get up late in the morning ★ The left part is "忄". 懒 and 赖(lài) have the same beginning sound l.	懒		
拼	② pīn　*v.* put together 拼音 phoneticize　拼命 risk one's life, defy death ★ The left part is "手". 拼 and 并 have similar pronunciation.	拼		
司	② sī　*v.* manage；similar to 后 and 同；same sound as 思 司机 driver ★ The part of the character is "口". The character means to order, charge or control.	司		
套	② tào　*v.* cover with；*n.* cover；*mw* [*measure word for books, furniture, rooms, etc.*]　外套 coat　笔套 cap of a pen　套装 suit　★ The big （"大"）on the top could cover the long （"镸"）at the bottom.	套		
央	② yāng　*n.* center 中央 center, middle ★ The character originally looked like a person standing at the center.	央		

生词 NEW WORDS

跟 gēn：follow

被 bèi：by (*used in the passive voice*)

书写 WRITING

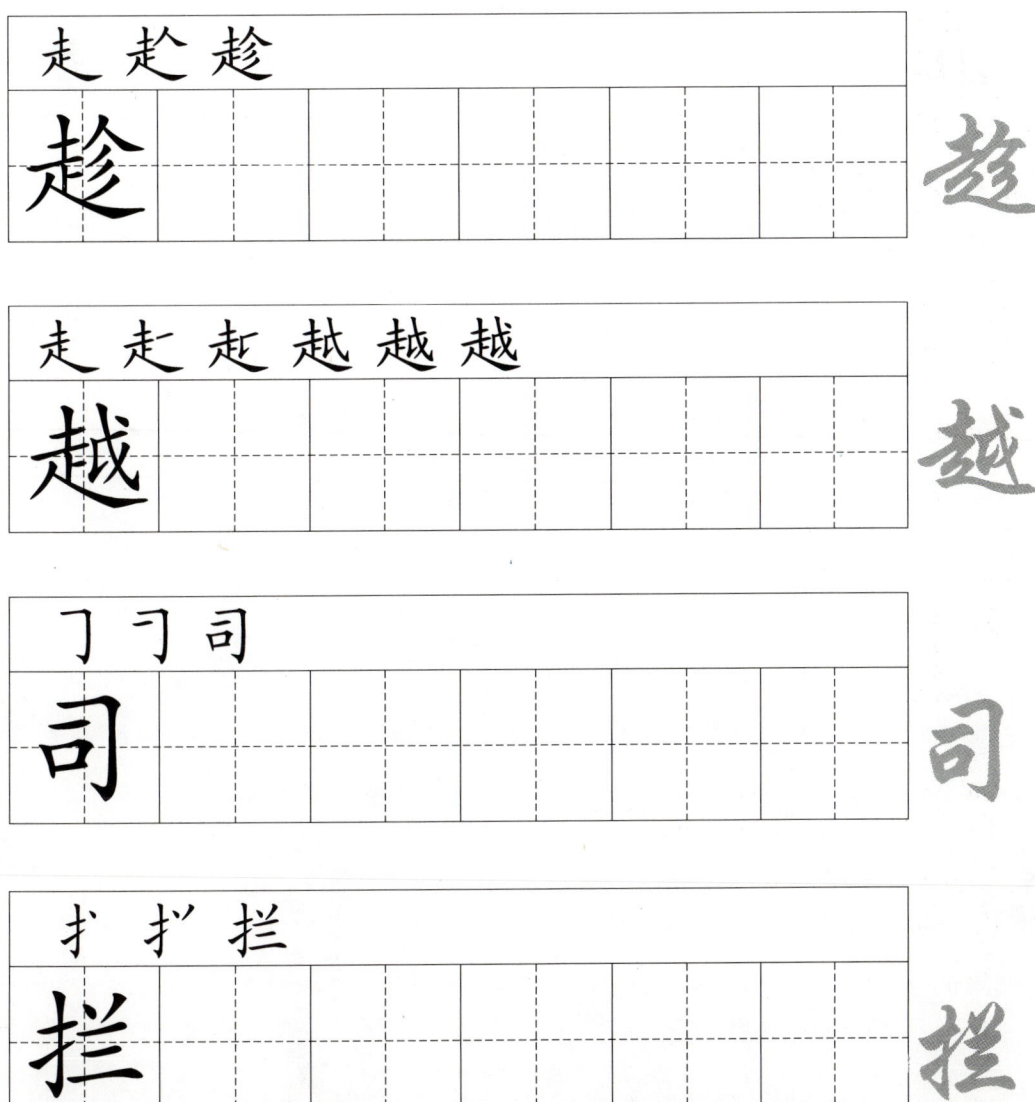

大　太　本　本　套　套　套　套

套　　　　　　　　　　　　　　　套

丶　冂　口　央　央

央　　　　　　　　　　　　　　央

足

课文 TEXT

踢足球

东东很顽皮，走起路来不是跑就是跳。他最喜欢踢足球，哪怕是一块石头，他也会把它踢来踢去。所以，一双鞋到他脚上没几天就破了，要么脚趾头出来了，要么脚后跟出来了。有一次，他跟同学们一起踢足球，从距离很远的地方射门，没想到一脚用力过大，连球带鞋一同飞到马路上去了。东东只好光着一只脚，一蹦一跳地跑到马路边去捡球。马路上人来车往，他站在那里，看不到球在哪儿，于是先蹲下找，接着又跪下找，最后就趴在地上找。他跨过人行道，终于在马路对面的车站旁找到了球。于是，他就用一只光脚想把球再踢回去。谁知他用力一踢，不但那只光脚很疼，而且球的方向也改变了，最后飞到了汽车轮子的底下，被压破了。他的脚也踩空了，跌了一跤，摔倒在地上。

91

部首 RADICAL　足 zú

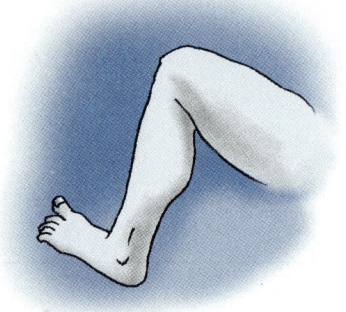

★ The character originally looked like a leg with a foot. Used as a radical, it is related to feet, road, action of feet, etc. and usually written on the left. It has the same meaning as "辶", "止", "走", "彳", "疋", "夂", etc. and is also used as a sound part.

书写 WRITING

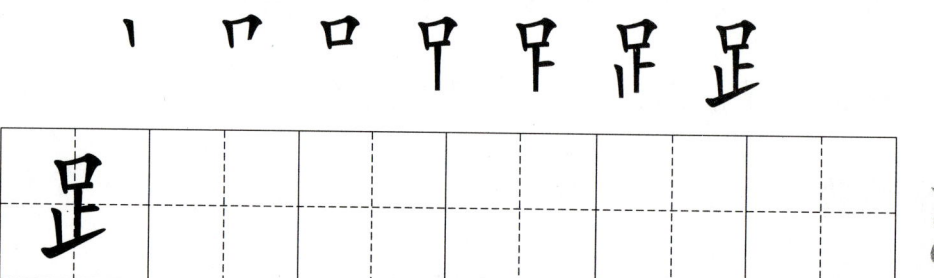

生字 NEW CHARACTERS

课文中的足部字

蹦	④ bèng　*v.* jump, leap similar to 山 and 月 ★ 蹦 and 崩 (bēng) differ only in tone.	蹦		
踩	② cǎi　*v.* step on ★ 踩 and 采 (cǎi) have the same pronunciation.	踩		
跌	② diē　*v.* fall down 跌跤 / 跌倒 trip and fall ★ 跌 and 失 had similar sound in ancient times.	跌		

蹲	② dūn *v.* squat ★ 蹲 and 尊(zūn) have the same ending sound uen.	蹲		
跟	① gēn *n.* heel; *v.* follow; similar to 很, 痕 and 眼 跟班 foot man of an official; join a reqular shift (or class) ★ 跟 and 艮(gèn) differ only in tone.	跟		
跪	② guì *v.* kneel 下跪 kneel down ★ 跪 and 危(wēi) have the same ending sound uei.	跪		
跤	jiāo *n.* fall 跌跤 trip and fall 摔跤 trip and fall, wrestle ★ 跤 and 交 have the same pronunciation.	跤		
距	② jù *n.* distance; same sound as 句 and 俱 距离 distance ★ 距 and 巨(jù) have the same pronunciation.	距		
跨	② kuà *v.* stride, straddle 跨栏 hurdle race ★ 跨 and 夸 (kuā) differ only in tone.	跨		
路	① lù *n.* road, way, path 马路 wide road, street 高速(sù)公路 highway ★ 路 and 各 had similar sound in ancient times.	路		
趴	③ pā *v.* bend over ★ 趴 and 八 have the same ending sound a.	趴		
跑	① pǎo *v.* run, leak, escape 跑步 jog, run ★ 跑 and 包 have the same ending sound ao.	跑		
踢	① tī *v.* kick 踢足球 play football ★ 踢 and 易(yì) have the same ending sound i.	踢		

跳	① tiào　*v.* jump; similar to 姚 跳舞 dance　　跳高 high jump　　跳远 long jump ★ 跳 and 兆(zhào) have the same ending sound ao.	跳		
趾	zhǐ　*n.* toe 脚趾 toe ★ 趾 and 止 have the same pronunciation.	趾		

课文中的其他生字

球 摔 顽	① qiú　*n.* ball; similar to 救 足球 football ★ At first it meant the round jade. 球 and 求 have the same pronunciation.	球		
	② shuāi　*v.* break, throw, fall 摔跤 trip and fall, wrestle ★ 摔 and 率 differ only in tone.	摔		
	(頑) ③ wán　*adj.* stupid, dense; similar to 远 顽皮 naughty ★ The right part is "页", meaning head. 顽 and 元 have the same ending sound an.	顽		

■ 生词　NEW WORDS

射 shè：shoot ［射门 shoot at the goal］

终于 zhōngyú：at last

轮子 lúnzi：wheel

底 dǐ：bottom

■ 书写　WRITING

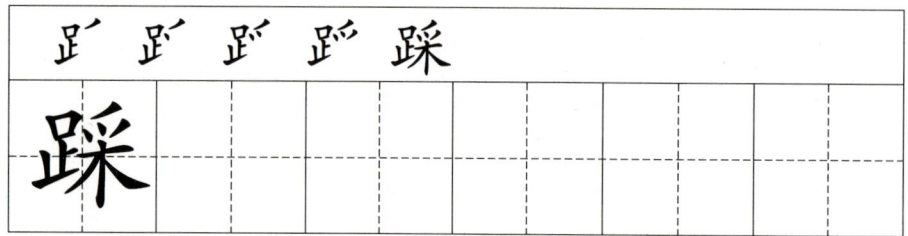

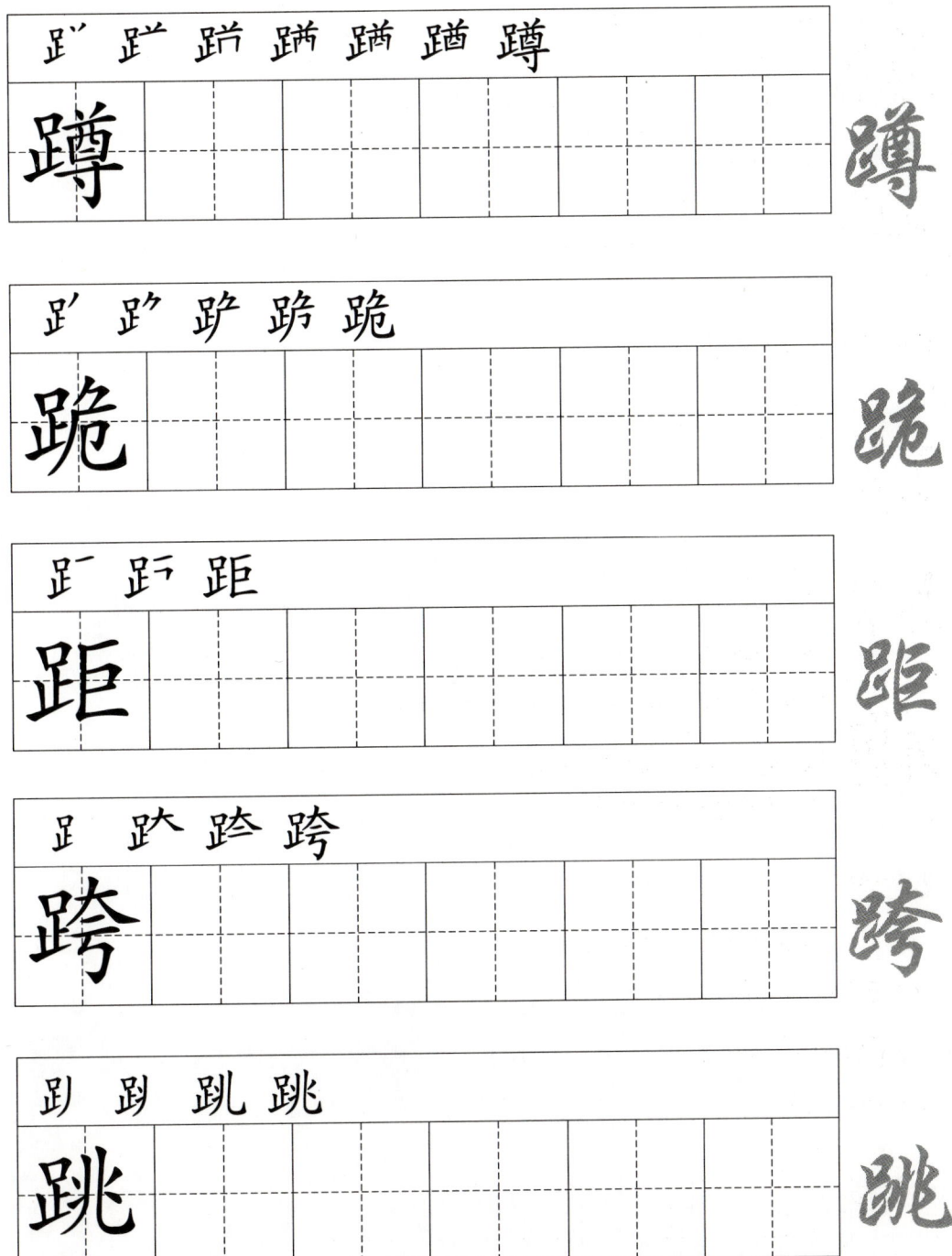

UNIT

2

第2单元

与自然有关（上）
Nature Related（I）

第17课 日部 Sun 🔘 17

■ 课文 TEXT

早晨·春天

　　早晨是一天的开始，春天是一年的开始。"一日之计在于晨，一年之计在于春"是中国的一句老话，意思是说：一天当中早晨最重要，一年当中春天最重要。因为春天越来越暖和，普遍对农业生产有好处；而昨天休息了一个晚上，第二天早晨起来，人的精神也会明显变好。但是，喜欢在晚上做事的人也很多，因为那时特别安静。

　　天晴的日子里，阳光普照，让人心情舒畅。如果是早晨天还比较暗的时候，或是傍晚黄昏，你还能看到星星与太阳互相映照，这种景色也特别美。

部首 RADICAL 日 rì

★ The character originally looked like the sun. Used as a radical, it is related to sun, light, brightness, warmness, dryness, time, weather, etc.

生字 NEW CHARACTERS

课文中的日部字

暗	② àn *adj.* dark, hidden; same sound as 按 昏暗 dim, dusky ★ 暗 and 音 had similar sound in ancient times.	暗	
晨	① chén *n.* morning 早晨 morning ★ 晨 and 辰(chén) have the same pronunciation.	晨	
春	① chūn *n.* spring 春天 spring　春节 Spring Festival ★ Originally it was written as "旾", having the same ending sound uen as "屯(tún)".	春	
昏	② hūn *adj.* dark, dim, confused; same sound as 婚 黄昏 dusk　昏暗 dim, dusky ★ "氏" looks like a root. Together with "日" it means sunset.	昏	
景	② jǐng *n.* view, situation; same sound as 警 风景 landscape ★ Originally it meant shadow from the sun. 景 and 京 differ only in tone.	景	
明	① míng *adj.* bright; same sound as 名 明天 tomorrow ★ The sun and the moon give us brightness day and night.	明	

暖	① nuǎn　*adj.* warm 暖和 warm　　温(wēn)暖 warm ★ 暖 and 爱(yuán) have the same ending sound an.	暖		
普	② pǔ　*adj.* general　普遍 universal, widespread, common 普照(zhào) shine on everything　普通 common ★ Originally it meant there is sunshine everywhere.	普		
晴	① qíng　*adj.* sunny similar to 请 and 睛；same sound as 情 晴天 sunny day ★ 晴 and 青 differ only in tone.	晴		
晚	① wǎn　*n.* evening；*adj.* late；similar to 兔 晚上 evening　晚会 evening party ★ 晚 and 免(miǎn) have the same ending sound an.	晚		
显	(顯) ② xiǎn　*adj.* apparent similar to 业 and 普 明显 obvious	显		
星	① xīng　*n.* star；similar to 性 and 姓 星期 week ★ 星 and 生 had similar sound in ancient times.	星		
阳	(陽) ① yáng　*n.* sun；*adj.* overt, positive 太阳 sun　阳光 sunshine ★ Originally it meant the south side of the mountain. "阝" meant mountain.	阳		
映	② yìng　*v.* reflect, shine 映照(zhào) shine upon ★ 映 and 央 (yāng) have the same beginning sound i.	映		
早	① zǎo　*adj.* early 早上/早晨 morning	早		
昨	① zuó　*n.* yesterday；similar to 作 昨天 yesterday ★ 昨 and 乍(zhà) had similar sound in ancient times.	昨		

课文中的其他生字

傍	② bàng *v.* be close to, draw near 傍晚 toward evening, at nightfall, at dusk ★傍 and 旁 have the same ending sound ɑng.	傍
遍	① biàn *n.* all over; same sound as 变 走遍 go everywhere 遍地 everywhere ★ The outside part is "辶" which is related to walking. Taken together it means everywhere. 遍 and 扁 (biǎn) differ only in tone.	遍
或	① huò *conj.* or, either 或者 or 或许 maybe ★ "戈" means weapon and "口" means place. Originally the two parts together meant protecting a place or the country.	或

生词 NEW WORDS

阳 yáng：sun, male ［太阳 sun   阳光 sunshine］

照 zhào：shine, reflect

书写 WRITING

旦 尸 尸 尸 晨 晨 晨

晨   晨

三 声 夫 春

春   春

一 厂 厍 氏 昏

昏

日 旷 昤 昤 暖

暖

丷 丷 丼 并 並 普

普

阝 阝 阳

阳

户 户 扁 扁 扁 遍

遍

昏

暖

普

阳

遍

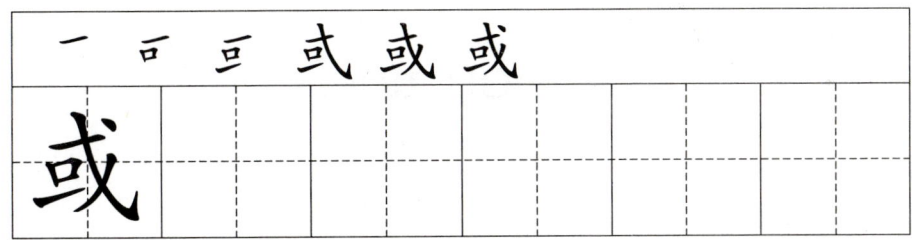

书写以前学过的字 Writing the characters you have learned before

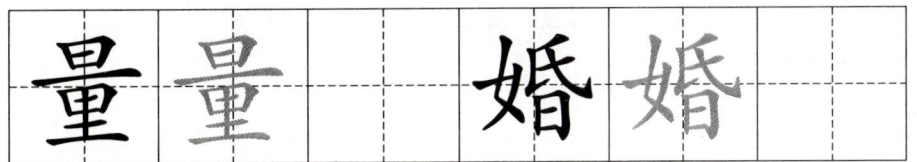

月

■ 课文 TEXT

月亮

在中国，每当月亮圆(yuán)的时候，人们经常会想起自己

的家乡和亲人，所以，中秋节(jié)晚上，一家人总是要在一

起望月亮，吃月饼(bǐng)。晴朗的夜空(kōng)，明亮的月光，满(mǎn)天的

星斗，会给人很多想象。人们对着月亮许下自己的愿望，

期待着、希望着它能实现(shí xiàn)。清(qīng)晨，当一轮(lún)朝阳升起的时

候，也许你还能看到那朦胧的月光。你会朝着明大走去，

你会朝着希望走去，你会朝着胜利(lì)走去。

诗歌里常有月亮，恋爱中的人喜欢月亮，而失恋的

人又会因为它产生悲伤、愁闷的感觉。

104

部首 RADICAL 月 yuè

★ The character originally looked like a moon. Used as a radical, it is related to moon, light, brightness, time, etc., and usually written on the right (see Lesson 7 "肉（月）"). It is also used as a sound part.

生字 NEW CHARACTERS

课文中的月部字

朗	② lǎng *adj.* bright, loud and clear 朗读 read aloud 晴朗 clear, sunny, fine ★ Originally it meant bright moonlight. 朗 and 良 have the same ending sound ang.	朗	
胧	（朧）lóng 朦胧 dim, obscure ★ 胧 and 龙 have the same pronunciation.	胧	
朦	méng 朦胧 dim, obscure ★ 朦 and 蒙（méng）have the same pronunciation.	朦	
期	① qī *n.* period of time; same sound as 七 and 妻 星期 week 期待 expect ★ 期 and 其 differ only in tone.	期	
望	① wàng *n.* full moon; *v.* look over; same sound as 忘 愿望 desire 希望 hope ★ 望 and 亡 differ only in tone.	望	
朝	① zhāo *n.* early morning; cháo *prep.* towards similar to 掉; same sound as 招 朝阳 rising sun ★ Originally it meant that the sun is rising, and the moon is setting down.	朝	

课文中的其他生字

爱	（愛）① ài　*v.* love, like 爱人 husband or wife, sweetheart　爱情 love 爱好 fondness, hobby　爱护 take good care of	爱
悲	② bēi　*adj.* sad, sorrowful；same sound as 杯 悲伤 sadness, sorrow ★ 悲 and 非 have the same ending sound ei.	悲
愁	② chóu　*adj.* worry, be anxious 愁闷 feel gloomy, be depressed 发愁 be anxious, worry	愁
待	② dài　*v.* treat, deal with；dāi　*v.* stay 对待 treat　期待 expect, hope　等(děng)待 wait for 待着 stay	待
恋	（戀）② liàn　*v.* love, long for 恋爱 be in love　恋人 sweetheart, lover 失恋 be disappointed in love ★ 恋 and 峦(luán) have the same ending sound an.	恋
闷	（悶）③ mèn　*adj.* bored, tightly closed；mēn　*adj.* stuffy, close　闷闷不乐 depressed, in low spirits ★ The heart is closed in the door. 闷 and 门 differ only in tone.	闷
诗	（詩）① shī　*n.* poem 诗歌 poem, verse　诗人 poet ★ 诗 and 寺(sì) have the same ending sound -i.	诗
希	① xī　*v.* hope similar to 布；same sound as 西 and 吸 希望 hope	希

生词 NEW WORDS

圆 yuán：round, circular

夜空 yèkōng：night sky

满 mǎn：full［满天 all over the sky］

实现 shíxiàn：realize, come true

清 qīng：clear ［清晨 early morning］

轮 lún：*measure word for the sun or the moon*

■ 书写 WRITING

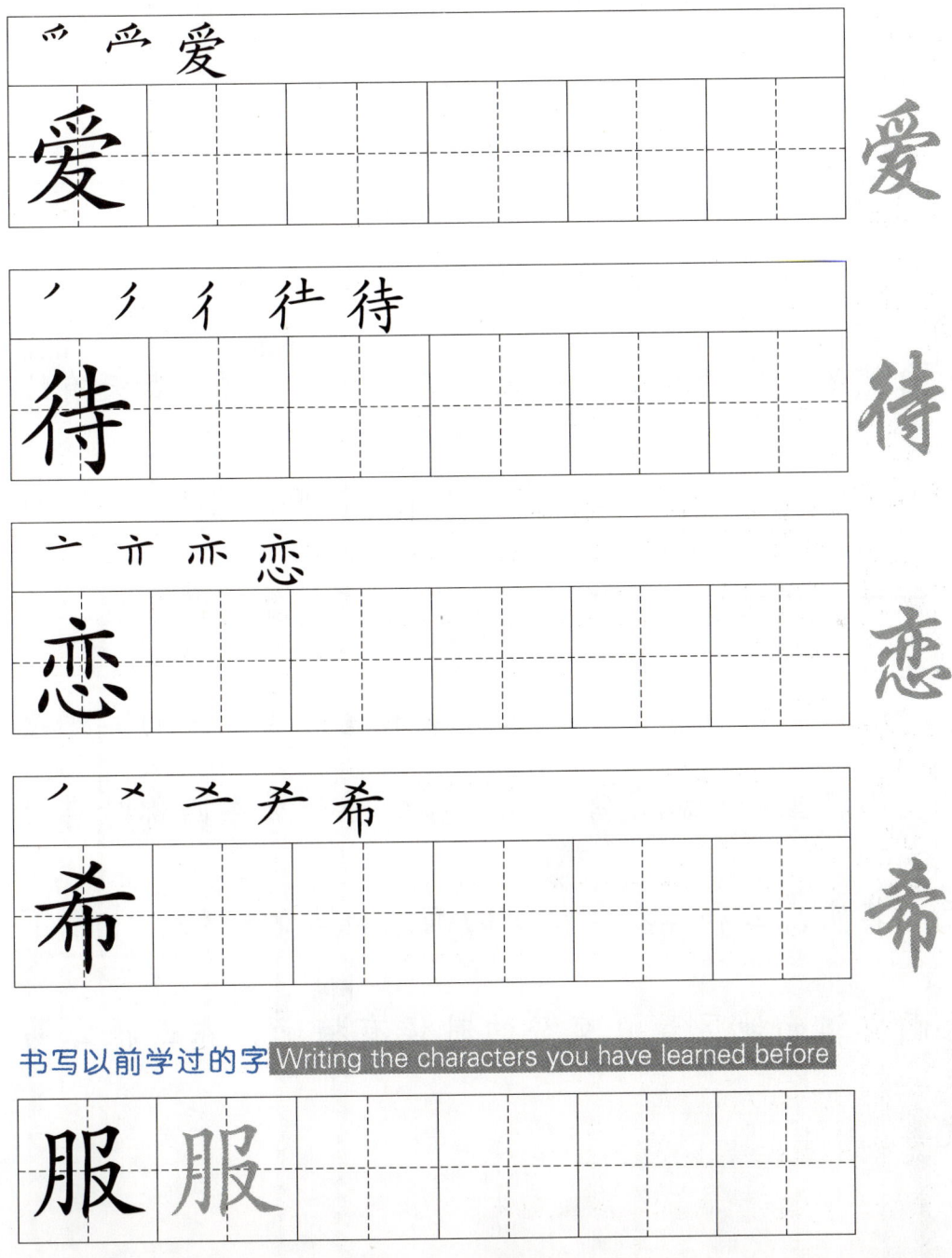

书写以前学过的字 Writing the characters you have learned before

第19课 雨部 Rain 19

课文 TEXT

虽然大多数人不喜欢下雨，但大地需要雨水，它是大自然给我们的礼物。雨也会变成很多花样：春天有绵（huā）（mián）绵的细雨（mián）（xì），夏天有雷雨，秋天有露水和霜，到了冬天（dōng），雪花飘飘（huā），到处是一片银白的景色（yín），而气温到了零度以下（dù）就会结冰（jié bīng）。还有雾，最让人捉摸不透：马路上的雾就是云，山腰里的云就是雾。在云雾中，什么东西都时有时无。其实，云和雾都是细小的雨（xì）。地震的时候，常常下大雨。江南地区春夏交替的时候有梅雨（jiāng）（méi），东西很容易发霉。

部首 RADICAL 雨 yǔ

罘 丽雨 雨 雨

★ The character originally looked like raining. Used as a radical, it is related to rain, weather, etc. It is usually written on the top and called "yǔzìtóu". It is also used as a sound part.

书写 WRITING

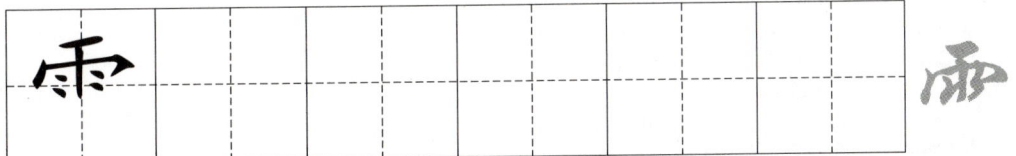

生字 NEW CHARACTERS

课文中的雨部字

雷	② léi　*n.* thunder 打雷 thunder　雷雨 thunderstorm, thundershower ★ Originally, the bottom part was "畾", like thunder.	雷	
零	① líng　*num.* zero; similar sound to 领 零度(dù) 0°, zero degree ★ Originally it meant raining continuously. 零 and 令 differ only in tone.	零	
露	② lù　*n.* dew 露水 dew ★ 露 and 路 have the same sound.	露	

霉	③ méi v. mildew, go moldy 发霉 go moldy ★ 霉 and 每 differ only in tone.	霉		
霜	③ shuāng n. frost, frostlike powder similar to 想; same sound as 双 ★ 霜 and 相 have the same ending sound ang.	霜		
雾	(霧) ② wù n. fog ★ 雾 and 务(wù, Lesson 47) have the same sound.	雾		
需	① xū v. need; similar to 而; same sound as 须 需要 need ★ 需 and 雨 have the same ending sound ü.	需		
雪	① xuě n. snow similar to 妇 and 扫 下雪 snow 雪花(huā) snowflake	雪		
震	③ zhèn v. shake, shock; similar to 晨 地震 earthquake ★ Originally it meant thundering. 震 and 辰 (chén) have the same ending sound en.	震		

课文中的其他生字

礼	(禮) ① lǐ n. ceremony, etiquette 礼物(wù) gift ★The left part is "示" which is related to God or ghost.	礼		
飘	(飄) ② piāo v. wave to and fro, float ★ The right part is "风" which is related to wind. 飘 and 票(piào) differ only in tone.	飘		
容	② róng v. allow, contain 内容 content 容易 easy ★ The top part "宀" means a house, and the bottom part "谷" means valley. The two parts together mean that a big house can contain much more things.	容		

替	② tì *v.* replace, take the place of 交替 supersede, replace 代替 replace, substitute 替换 replace, displace ★ "夫" means a person. Double "夫" mean one can take the place of another.	替		
透	② tòu *v.* pass through, appear 捉摸不透 cannot find clearly ★ The outside part is "辶", meaning "pass through". 透 and 秀(xiù) have similar sound at the end.	透		
温	② wēn *adj.* warm; *n.* temperature 气温 air temperature 温暖 warm 温度(dù) temperature ★ Originally it meant warm water.	温		
易	② yì *v.* exchange, change; *adj.* easy 容易 easy 交易 business	易		
捉	② zhuō *v.* catch, grasp 捉摸 guess, expect ★ The left part is "手". 捉 and 足 had similar sound in ancient times.	捉		

生词 NEW WORDS

花样 huāyàng：variety, trick

绵绵 miánmián：continuous，unbroken

细 xì：thin, slender［细雨 drizzle, mizzle   细小 very small, tiny］

银 yín：silver

结冰 jié bīng：ice over, ice up

书写 WRITING

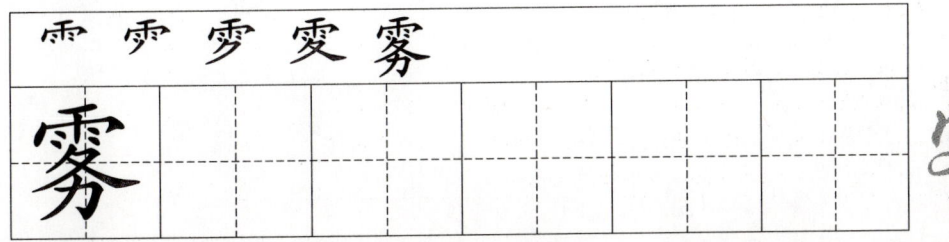

霄 雩 霒 霹 霆 霆 震 震

震

` ラ ネ ネ 礼

礼

禾 秀 秀 透

透

震

礼

透

水

■ 课文 TEXT

fàn
一饭一汤

tiáo
中国有两条大河：北面是黄河，水比较浅，有许多泥沙；南面是长江，水比较深，也比较清。它们都是从西向东流到海洋。还有很多湖，散布在各个地方。水是生命的源泉，没有水就没有生命。我们要保护它，不要污染它。用水可以洗澡、洗衣服，游泳池里需要水，我们喝的汤也要用水。

běn fàn diàn
说到汤，有这么一个故事：有个中国人到日本饭店去
fàn
吃饭，他不懂日文，但觉得日语也用汉字，意思差不
fàn   wù
多，于是就写了"一饭一汤"四个字。不一会儿，服务
wǎn fàn   wǎn rè   fàn
员拿来一碗饭和满满一碗热水。他吃了以后，觉得饭的
diǎn
味道还不错，可汤不浓，味道很淡，而且一点儿油也没
有，就像白开水一样。他不知道，日文的"汤"和汉语古
rè
文的意思一样，就是热水！

113

■ 部首 RADICAL　水（氵）shuǐ

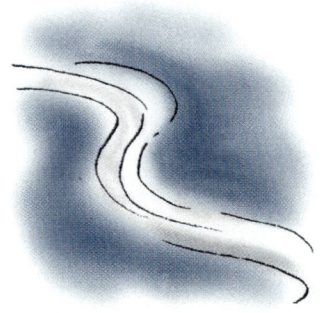

★ The character originally looked like a river with some drops of water. Used as a radical, it is related to river, water, liquid, etc. Written on the left, it is changed to "氵" which is called "sāndiǎnshuǐ".

■ 书写 WRITING

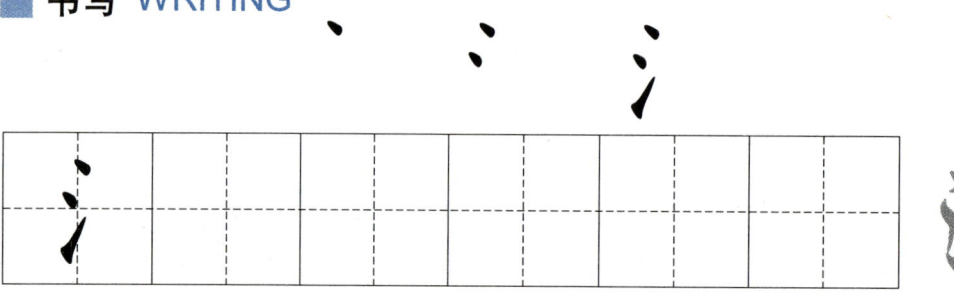

■ 生字 NEW CHARACTERS

课文中的水部字

池	② chí　*n.* pool same sound as 迟 and 持；similar to 地 游泳池 swimming pool　　电池 battery	池	
淡	② dàn　*adj.* light, thin, tasteless similar to 谈；same sound as 但 and 旦 ★ 淡 and 炎(yán) have the same ending sound an.	淡	
海	① hǎi　*n.* sea 大海 sea　　上海 Shanghai ★ 海 and 每 had similar sound in ancient times.	海	
汉	(漢) ① hàn　*n.* name of river, Chinese (language) 汉语 Chinese language　★ Originally it meant the Han river, later it came to mean the place, the nation and the language. 汉 and 叹(tàn) have the same ending sound an.	汉	

114

河	① hé *n.* river; same sound as 何 and 和 黄河 Yellow River ★ 河 and 可 have the same ending sound e.	河		
湖	① hú *n.* lake 西湖 West Lake (in Hangzhou) ★ 湖 and 胡 have the same pronunciation.	湖		
江	① jiāng *n.* river; same sound as 姜 长江 Yangtze River ★ 江 and 工 had similar sound in ancient times.	江		
流	① liú *v.* flow, drift; similar to 慌 and 育 流行 prevail ★ The top part on the right is the inverted "子" and the bottom is like amniotic fluid.	流		
满	(滿) ① mǎn *adj.* full; similar to 瞒 满意 satisfaction ★ Originally it meant "full of water". 满 and 瞒 (mán) differ only in tone.	满		
泥	② ní *n.* mud; similar to 呢 泥土 clay, soil, earth 水泥 cement ★ 泥 and 尼(ní) have the same pronunciation.	泥		
浓	(濃) ② nóng *adj.* dense, thick, great, strong ★ 浓 and 农 have the same pronunciation.	浓		
浅	(淺) ① qiǎn *adj.* shallow, light similar to 钱 ★ 浅 and 戋(jiān) have the same ending sound ian.	浅		
清	① qīng *adj.* clear; similar to 情, 晴, 请, 睛, 精 and 静 清楚(chu) clear ★ Originally it meant clear water. 清 and 青 have the same pronunciation.	清		
泉	④ quán *n.* spring 泉水 spring 源泉 headspring, fountainhead 喷(pēn)泉 fountain ★ The top part is "白". The character means clean water from spring.	泉		

染	② rǎn　*v.* dye　　染料(liào) dyestuff, dye　　污染 pollute, contaminate　　★ The right part originally was "朵" meaning flower. Flowers of different colors put in water could be used as dye.	染		
沙	② shā　*n.* sand; similar to 妙 沙子 sand　　沙滩(tān) sand beach ★ 沙 and 少 have the same beginning sound sh.	沙		
深	① shēn　*adj.* deep, dark same sound as 身 ★ 深 and 琛(chēn) have the same ending sound en.	深		
汤	(湯) ① tāng　*n.* soup, hot water; similar to 肠 and 扬 ★ Originally it meant hot water. 汤 and 杨 or 扬(yáng) have the same ending sound ang.	汤		
污	② wū　*n.* dirty 污染 pollute, contaminate ★ 污 and 亏 (originally written as "于") had similar sound in ancient times.	污		
洗	① xǐ　*v.* wash 洗澡 take a shower ★ 洗 and 先 have the same beginning sound x.	洗		
洋	② yáng　*n.* ocean 海洋 ocean　　太平洋 Pacific　　大西洋 Atlantic ★ 洋 and 羊 have the same pronunciation.	洋		
泳	① yǒng　*n.* swim 游泳 swim ★ 泳 and 永 have the same pronunciation.	泳		
油	② yóu　*n.* oil; same sound as 尤 and 游 汽油 gasoline ★ 油 and 由 have the same pronunciation.	油		
游	① yóu　*v.* swim, travel; same sound as 由 and 尤 游泳 swim　　旅游 tour ★ 游 and 斿(yóu) have the same pronunciation.	游		

| 源 | ② yuán *n.* source, fountain；similar to 愿

源泉 fountainhead, headspring

★ 源 and 原(yuán) have the same pronunciation. | 源 | | |
| 澡 | ① zǎo *n.* bath

洗澡 have a bath, take a shower

★ 澡 and 枣(zǎo) have the same pronunciation. | 澡 | | |

课文中的其他生字

| 代 | ① dài *n.* generation, era；*v.* act for
similar to 找 and 试
古代 ancient 代替 replace, substitute for 代表 delegate | 代 | | |
| 散 | ① sàn *v.* break up, disperse, distribute

散步 take a walk 散布 spread 分散 disperse, scatter | 散 | | |

书写 WRITING

氵 氵 泸 泸 泸 流 流							
流							

流

氵 汁 满							
满							

满

氵　氵　沪　沪　泮　浅　浅

浅

氵　氵　沪　沪　深

深

氵　氵　汤　汤　汤

汤

氵　氵　污

污

亻　亻　仁　代　代

代

一　十　艹　艹　肯　散

散

浅

深

汤

污

代

散

氵	汩	洞	洞	温	温			

温								

温

书写以前学过的字 Writing the characters you have learned before

没	没		活	活	
酒	酒		法	法	
注	注				

■ 课文 **TEXT**

不怕冷

妈妈问小明长大了准备做什么，小明说："我决定长

大后去一次南极。"妈妈说："南极很冷，到处都是冰雪，

天寒地冻。你不怕吗？"小明说："这种情况我知道，所

以，我已经作好了准备：我决心从今天起，尽量每天吃

一根冰棍，冬天也吃，到那时就不怕冷了。同时，我要

多吃凉拌菜和果冻。还有，我要停止减肥，因为胖的人

不怕冷。您不是说那里是冰天雪地吗？而且听说那里的

冰雪是很干净的，所以，渴了可以喝，还可以把它化开

了冲咖啡，真是享受啊！"

部首 RADICAL 　冫 bīng

★ The character originally looked like ice. Used as a radical, it is related to ice, cold, etc. The meaning is similar to "氵". Usually it is written on the left and called "liǎngdiǎnshuǐ".

书写 WRITING

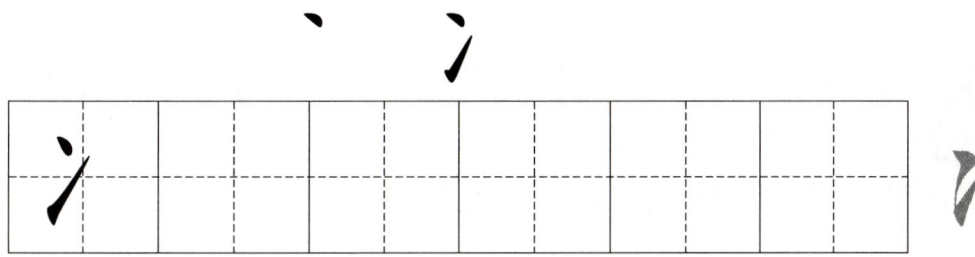

生字 NEW CHARACTERS

课文中的冫部字

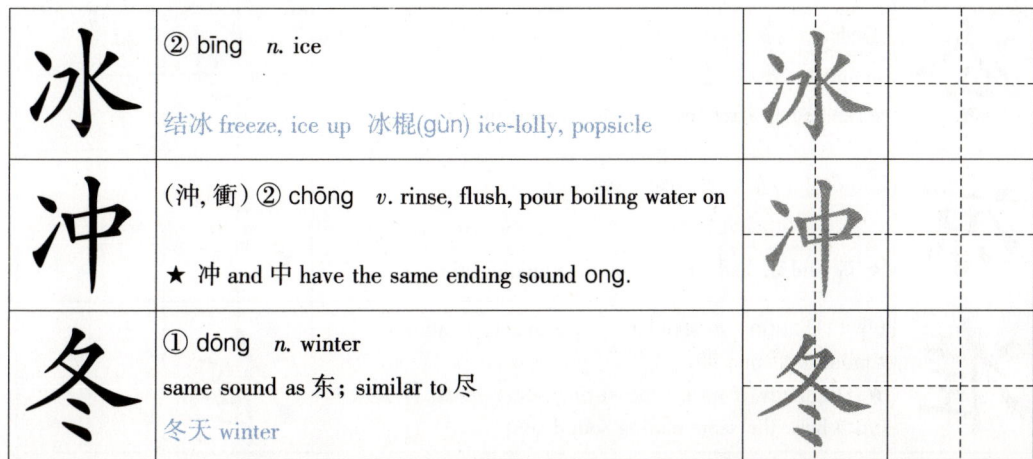

冰	② bīng　*n.* ice 结冰 freeze, ice up　冰棍(gùn) ice-lolly, popsicle	冰
冲	(沖, 衝) ② chōng　*v.* rinse, flush, pour boiling water on ★ 冲 and 中 have the same ending sound ong.	冲
冬	① dōng　*n.* winter same sound as 东；similar to 尽 冬天 winter	冬

冻	（凍）② dòng　*v.* freeze；*n.* jelly 果冻 jelly ★ 冻 and 东 differ only in tone.	冻		
寒	① hán　*adj.* cold 寒假 (jià) winter vacation　寒冷 cold　★ The top part "宀" represents a house, the middle looks like two hands holding dried grass to put on the bed.	寒		
减	（減）② jiǎn　*v.* decrease, minus, reduce similar to 喊 and 感；same sound as 捡　减肥 loose weight ★ 减 and 咸(xián) have the same ending sound ian.	减		
尽	（盡）② jìn　*v.* finish, exhaust　　尽 (jǐn) 量 reach the limit　尽情 as much as one likes　　★ The character originally had a hand holding a brush on the top, water in the middle, and a plate at the bottom. Taken together it meant to wash plate after eating.	尽		
净	（净）① jìng　*adj.* clean, complete；same sound as 静 干净 clean ★ 净 and 争 had similar sound in ancient times.	净		
决	（決）① jué　*v.* burst, decide similar to 映 and 快；same sound as 觉 决定(dìng) decide　决心 decision　★ Originally it meant flood water bursting out of the dykes.	决		
况	（況）① kuàng　*n.* situation, condition 情况 situation ★ 况 and 兄had similar sound in ancient times.	况		
冷	① lěng　*adj.* cold similar to 领 and 零 ★ 冷 and 令 have the same beginning sound l.	冷		
凉	① liáng　*adj.* cool；same sound as 量 凉拌菜(cài) cold dish ★ 凉 and 京 had similar sound in ancient times.	凉		
准	（準）① zhǔn　*n.* standard；*adj.* exact；*v.* allow similar to 谁 and 推　　准备(bèi) prepare ★ Originally it meant measuring water level. 準 and 隼 (sǔn) have the same ending sound uen.	准		

课文中的其他生字

拌	④ bàn　*v.* mix；same sound as 伴 凉拌菜(cài) cold dish ★ The left part is "手". 拌 and 半 have the same pronunciation.	拌
咖	① kā 咖啡 coffee ★ 咖 and 加 (jiā, Lesson 47) have the same ending sound a.	咖
啡	① fēi 咖啡 coffee ★ 啡 and 非 have the same pronunciation.	啡
极	（極）① jí　*adv.* extremely, in the extreme 南极 South Pole　　好极了 excellent ★ 极 and 及 have the same pronunciation.	极
渴	① kě　*adj.* thirsty；similar to 喝 口渴 thirsty　　渴望 long for ★ 渴 and 曷(hé) have the same ending sound e.	渴

■ **生词** NEW WORDS

根 gēn：root [*measure word for something like stick*]

享受：enjoy

■ **书写** WRITING

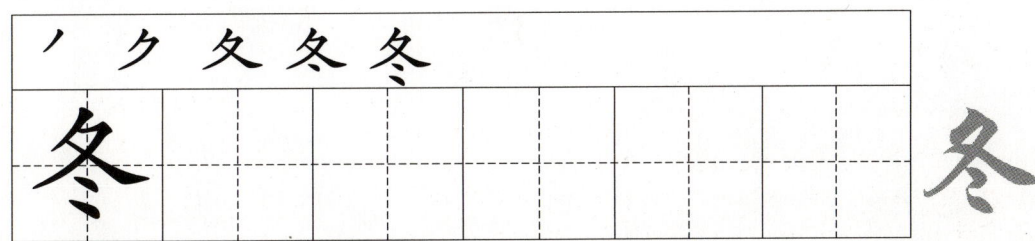

冫 冫 冫 冱 减

减 减

冫 冫 冫 冲 决

决 决

冫 冫 冫 准 准

准 准

冫 冫 冫 渴 渴 渴

渴 渴

第22课 火部 Fire 22

■ 课文 TEXT

火

　　火的发明是人类(lèi)的一大进步。火可以用来点灯照明，可以用来暖和身体、防止(fáng)寒冷，可以把食品加热烧熟，可以把矿(kuàng)石烧炼成金属，火灭了以后的灰还可以用来做肥料(liào)。城里的人现在大多用煤和煤气来点火煮饭(fàn)、烤肉、煎鱼、熬汤、炒鸡蛋(jī dàn)都要用火。然而，用火的时候如果不小心，也会引起爆炸与火灾，尤其是天气比较(jiào)干燥的时候。打仗时，枪(qiāng)和炮的子弹(dàn)里面装的都是火药(yào)。

■ 部首　RADICAL　火（灬）huǒ

★ The character originally looked like fire. Used as a radical, it is related to fire, light, brightness, temperature, weapon, etc. Written at the bottom, it is changed to "灬" which is called "sìdiǎndǐ". It is also used as a sound part.

■ 书写　WRITING

丶　 丶丶　 丷丶　 灬

| 灬 | | | | | | | 灬 |

■ 生字　NEW CHARACTERS

课文中的火部字

熬	③ áo　 *v.* cook on a slow fire, boil, endure; similar to 放 熬夜 stay up late (or all night) ★ 熬 and 敖(áo) have the same pronunciation.	熬	
爆	③ bào　 *v.* explode, burst 爆炸 explode　 爆竹 firecracker ★ 爆 and 暴(bào) have the same pronunciation.	爆	
炒	③ chǎo　 *v.* stir-fry, saute; same sound as 吵 炒面 chow mein ★ 炒 and 少 have the same ending sound ao.	炒	

灯	(燈) ① dēng *n.* lamp, light 电灯 electric light ★ 灯 and 丁 have the same beginning sound d.	灯		
点	(點) ① diǎn *n.* spot, dot, drop; *v.* light (a fire) 一点 a little 点灯 turn on the light 点火 light a fire ★ In the original character the left part was "黑". 点 and 占 have the same ending sound an.	点		
灰	② huī *n.* ash; *adj.* gray; same sound as 挥 ★ The top part is changed from "又", representing a hand. The bottom part represents fire. Taken together it means the thing (ash) that hands can safely touch after the fire is extinguished.	灰		
煎	③ jiān *v.* fry, decoct same sound as 肩 ★ 煎 and 前 have the same ending sound ian.	煎		
烤	② kǎo *v.* bake similar to 老 and 教 ★ 烤 and 考 (kǎo) have the same pronunciation.	烤		
炼	(煉) ① liàn *v.* refine, temper; similar to 冻 锻炼 take exercise ★ 炼(煉) and 柬(jiǎn) have the same ending sound ian.	炼		
煤	② méi *n.* coal 煤气 gas ★ 煤 and 某(mǒu) have the same beginning sound m.	煤		
灭	(滅) ② miè *v.* put out, destroy ★ It looks like putting out the fire by putting something on it.	灭		
炮	② pào *n.* big gun, cannon similar to 跑 ★ 炮 and 包 have the same ending sound ao.	炮		
热	(熱) ① rè *adj.* hot; *n.* heat 加热 heat 热情 enthusiasm, warmth 热爱 love ardently ★ 热 and 执(zhí) had similar sound in ancient times.	热		

烧	（燒）① shāo *v.* burn, cook 发烧 have a fever 烧饭(fàn) do the cooking ★ 烧 and 尧(yáo) have the same ending sound ao.	烧		
熟	① shú *adj.* cooked, ripe；similar to 享 and 丸 烧熟 cooked ★ 熟 and 孰(shú) have the same pronunciation.	熟		
灾	（災）② zāi *n.* calamity, disaster 火灾 fire 水灾 flood ★ The top part means a house. Taken together it means that the house is on fire.	灾		
燥	② zào *adj.* dry；same sound as 造 干燥 dry ★ 燥 and 杲(zào) have the same pronunciation.	燥		
炸	③ zhà *v.* burst, explode；zhá *v.* deep-fry similar to 作 and 昨 爆炸 blow up, explode ★ 炸 and 乍(zhà) have the same pronunciation.	炸		
照	① zhào *v.* shine, reflect, light up；similar to 招 and 绍 照相 take a photo 照明 illumination, lighting 按照 according to ★ 照 and 昭(zhāo) differ only in tone.	照		
煮	② zhǔ *v.* cook, boil；similar sound to 暑 煮饭(fàn) cook rice, cook a meal 煮鸡(jī) 蛋(dàn) boil eggs ★ 煮 and 者 had similar sound in ancient times.	煮		

课文中的其他生字

| 属 | ② shǔ   *v.* belong to, be born in Chinese animal year
属于 belong to   金属 metal   属马 be born in horse year
★ 属 and 禹(yǔ) have similar ending sound u and ü. | 属 | | |
| 仗 | ③ zhàng   *n.* battle
打仗 war, battle
★ 仗 and 丈 have the same pronunciation. | 仗 | | |

128

生词 NEW WORDS

类 lèi：kind ［人类 human being］

防止 fángzhǐ：prevent, avoid

矿石 kuàngshí：ore

肥料 féiliào：fertilizer

枪 qiāng：gun

子弹 zǐdàn：bullet

火药 huǒyào：gunpowder, powder

书写 WRITING

二	丰	圭	耂	考	敖	熬			
熬									

熬

火	炉	炉	焊	煜	煐	煐	爆	爆	
爆									

爆

一	ナ	灰							
灰									

灰

火　灯　灯　炉　炼　炼

炼

炼

火　灯　烘　焩　煤

煤

煤

火　炌　烊　烤　烧

烧

烧

尸　尸　居　居　属　属

属

属

书写以前学过的字 Writing the characters you have learned before

然　然

第23课 土部 Soil & Earth ◎ 23

■ 课文 TEXT

　　　　　　　　　　　　　　yīn
人们常常把土地比做母亲，因为它能生长出许多东

西。不仅如此，它还有许多其他用途：打地基，垒墙壁，
　　　　　　　　　　pèng
造房子……但是土碰到水会变湿，土做的墙也容易坏。

古代中国人在北方边境建起了长城，有的地方的长城就
　　　　　　zhuān
是用一块块的土砖堆起来的，现在已经看不到了。后来
　　　　　　　　　　　　　　　yìng　　　láo dù
人们发现，土砖用火烧过以后会变得坚硬，增加牢度，就
zhuān　　　　　　　　　　　　zhuān
用烧砖造房子，有钱人还用烧砖为自己造坟墓。现在的
　　　　　　　　　　　　shì
人开大会，都是在礼堂、在室内，会前会后都有人打扫

垃圾；古代的人都是直接坐在地上的，一块平坦的土地
　　　　　　　　　　　　　　　hu
就可以成为会场，满天尘土也不在乎。

131

■ 部首 RADICAL 土 tǔ

★ The character originally looked like soil. Used as a radical, it is related to soil, ground, landform, dust, building made of soil, etc. It is also used as a sound part of characters with the pronunciation tu or du.

■ 生字 NEW CHARACTERS

课文中的土部字

壁	② bì *n.* wall same sound as 必 and 闭；similar to 尸, 口 and 辛 墙壁 wall ★ 壁 and 辟(bì) have the same pronunciation.	壁		
场	(場) ① chǎng *n.* field, site; same sound as 厂；similar to 汤, 肠 and 扬 广场 square ★ 场(場) and 易(yáng) have the same ending sound ang.	场		
尘	(塵) ③ chén *n.* dust; same sound as 晨 灰尘 dust ★ The top part is "小". Taken together it means little soil.	尘		
堆	② duī *n.* heap, pile; similar to 推, 谁 and 准 堆放 pile up ★ 堆 and 隹(zhuī) have the same ending sound uei.	堆		
坟	(墳) ③ fén *n.* grave, tomb 坟墓 grave, tomb ★ 坟 and 文 have the same ending sound en.	坟		
坏	(壞) ① huài *adj.* bad；*v.* spoil 坏人 bad person ★ Things made by soil are spoiled easily.	坏		

132

基	① jī *n.* foundation, base；similar to 期 基础 base, foundation 地基 ground ★ 基 and 其 have the same ending sound i.	基		
圾	② jī similar to 吸；same sound as 基 垃圾 rubbish ★ 圾 and 及 differ only in tone.	圾		
坚	（堅）① jiān *adj.* firm, hard；same sound as 肩 and 煎 坚持 insist on 坚硬（yìng）hard, solid ★ 坚（堅）and 臤（qiān）have the same ending sound ian.	坚		
境	② jìng *n.* area, border；same sound as 净 边境 border ★ 境 and 竟（jìng）have the same pronunciation.	境		
块	（塊）① kuài *n.* block, piece, lump similar to 决；same sound as 快 ★ Originally it meant a piece (or a block) of soil.	块		
垃	② lā similar to 位；same sound as 拉 垃圾 rubbish ★ 垃 and 立 have the same beginning sound l.	垃		
垒	（壘）④ lěi *v.* build by piling up stones；*n.* base, rampart ★ 垒（壘）and 晶（lěi）have the same pronunciation.	垒		
墓	③ mù *n.* grave；similar to 摸；same sound as 木 and 目 坟墓 tomb, grave ★ 墓 and 莫（mò）have the same beginning sound m.	墓		
墙	（墙）① qiáng *n.* wall 墙壁 wall ★ The right part originally looked like a storehouse (to keep grain and food) surrounded by a wall made of soil.	墙		
坦	③ tǎn *adj.* broad and level, open, frank similar to 但 平坦 plainness ★ 坦 and 旦 have the same ending sound an.	坦		

| 堂 | ① táng *n.* hall; similar to 常
食堂 mess hall, canteen　礼堂 auditorium　大堂 lobby
★ 堂 and 尚 have the same ending sound ɑng. | 堂 | | |
| 增 | ① zēng *v.* add
增加 increase
★ 增 and 曾(zēng) have the same pronunciation. | 增 | | |

课文中的其他生字

| 湿 | （濕）② shī *adj.* wet, damp
★ The left part is "水". 湿 and 显 had similar sound in ancient times. | 湿 | | |
| 途 | ② tú *n.* road, way
用途 use　前途 future
★ 途 and 余 have the similar ending sound u and ü. | 途 | | |

■ 生词 NEW WORDS

碰 pèng：bump into, meet, touch

牢度 láodù：firmness

■ 书写 WRITING

土　圹　培　境							
境							

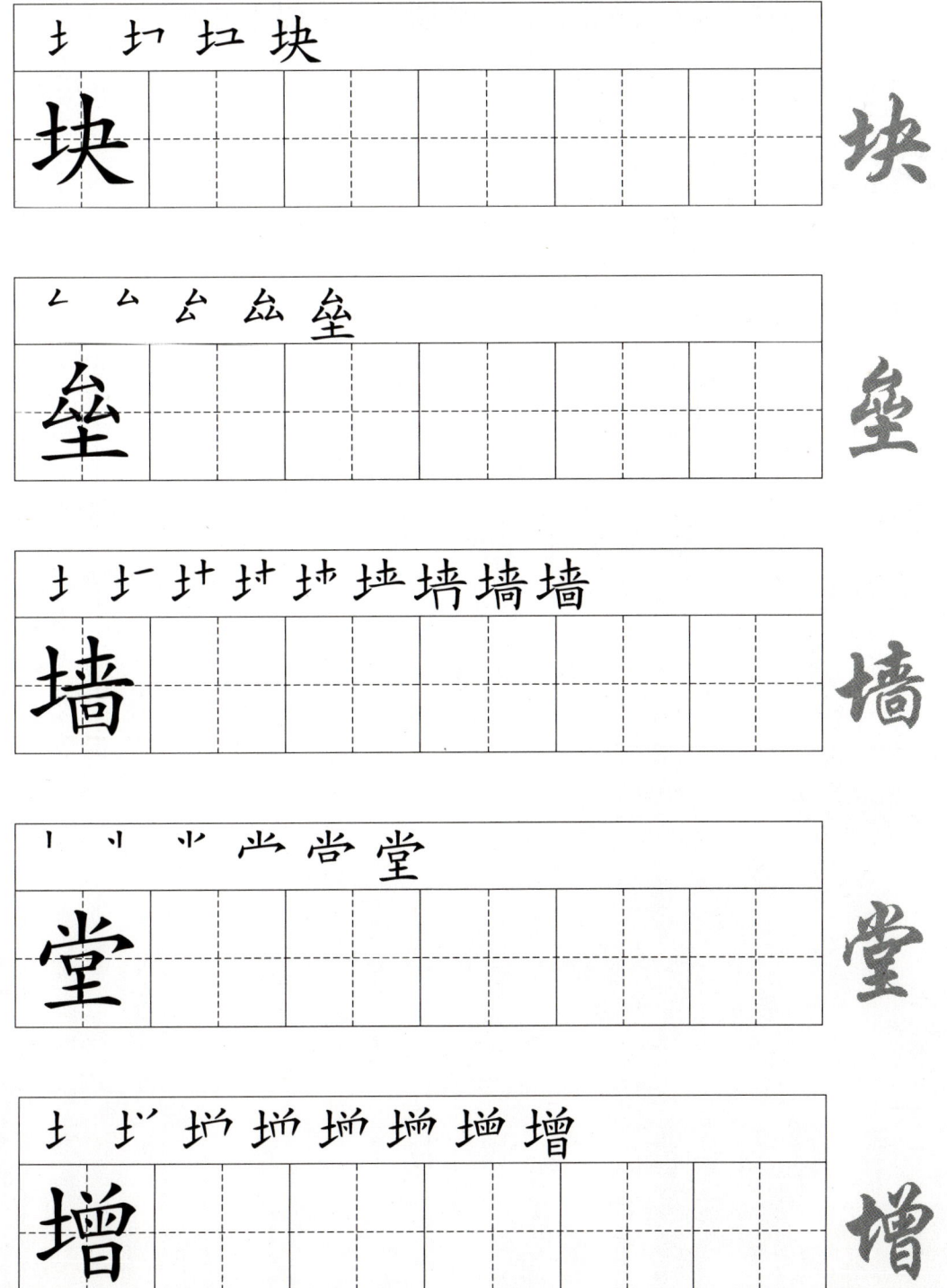

土 扌 圹 块						
块						

厶 厶 幺 幺 垒						
垒						

土 圹 圹 圹 圹 垆 墙 墙						
墙						

⺌ ⺌ 学 学 尚 堂						
堂						

土 圹 圹 圹 圹 圹 增						
增						

块

垒

墙

堂

增

书写以前学过的字 Writing the characters you have learned before

猜谜语 Riddles

bǎo
有样东西是个宝，垃圾堆里能找到。

(打一个字)

第 24 课 山部 Mountain 24

■ 课文 TEXT

山

　　有山就有水，山水总是相连的，水的边上就是岸，水底下的山露出了水面就是岛。山顶比较尖的又叫 dǐ "峰"，比较平一点的叫"岗"，山顶上有路可以通行的 jiào 叫"岭"。山路弯弯曲曲、坡度又陡、很难走的时候， dù dǒu 我们会说"山路崎岖"。大块的石头又叫岩石，如果山峰就是一大块石头，常常就叫什么岩。许多地名就是按照山的各种地形来命名的，比如：台湾岛、云岗、南岭、七星岩。

　　中国的很多山区以前经济都不太发达，不过，那是暂时的，人们会发现新的有价值的东西。目前，有不少山区已经在发展旅游业了。

部首 RADICAL 山 shān

★ The character originally looked like a mountain with three peaks. Used as a radical, it is related to mountain, landform, rock, etc. It is also used as a sound part of characters with the pronunciation an or ian.

生字 NEW CHARACTERS

课文中的山部字

岸	② àn　n. bank, shore ★ 岸 and 干 have the same ending sound an.	岸		
岛	(島) ② dǎo　n. island ★ It looked like the peak of mountain that came out of the lake or sea. 岛 and 鸟 have the same ending sound ao.	岛		
峰	③ fēng　n. peak, summit; same sound as 风 山峰 mountain peak ★ 峰 and 夆(fēng) have the same pronunciation.	峰		
岗	(崗) ③ gāng　n. hillock, mound ★ 岗 and 冈(岡 gāng) have the same pronunciation.	岗		
岭	(嶺) ④ lǐng　n. mountain range similar to 冷 and 零; same sound as 领 ★ 岭 and 令 differ only in tone.	岭		
崎	qí　adj. uneven 崎岖 rugged ★崎 and 奇(qí) have the same pronunciation.	崎		

| 岖 | (嶇) qū
崎岖 rugged
★ 岖 and 区 have the same pronunciation. | 岖 | | |
| 岩 | (巖) ③ yán *n.* crag, rock, cliff
岩石 rock
★ It means the rock is so big that it looks like a mountain. | 岩 | | |

课文中的其他生字

曾	② céng *adv.* once, ever, before；Zēng *n.* family name 曾经 once, ever ★ Originally it meant layer or floor, now we use "层(層)" to indicate this meaning.	曾		
济	(濟) ① jì *v.* cross a river, help；same sound as 既 经济 economic 救济 relieve, succor ★ 济 and 齐 have the same ending sound i.	济		
价	(價) ② jià *n.* price, value 价值 value, worth 价钱 price, cost ★ 价 and 介 have the same beginning sound j.	价		
尖	② jiān *adj.* pointed, sharp；*n.* tip, top similar to 尘；same sound as 肩, 坚 and 煎 ★ The top part is small, and the bottom is big. It looks like a pointed tip.	尖		
旅	① lǚ *n.* force, troops；*v.* travel 旅游 tour 旅行 travel, trip 旅馆(guǎn) hotel ★ The character originally looked like troops gathering under a flag.	旅		
难	(難) ① nán *adj.* difficult；nàn *n.* disaster, calamity, catastrophe 困(kùn)难 difficulty ★ 难(難) and 汉(漢 hàn) have the same ending sound an.	难		
坡	② pō *n.* slope；similar to 皮 and 疲 坡度(dù) slope grade, gradient ★ 坡 and 皮 have the same beginning sound p.	坡		

139

台	（臺）② tái *n.* station, stage, platform similar to 始；same sound as 抬 台湾 Taiwan　电视台 TV station　舞台 stage	台		
湾	（灣）④ wān *n.* bay 台湾 Taiwan ★ 湾 and 弯 have the same pronunciation.	湾		
形	② xíng *n.* form, shape; same sound as 行 地形 landform, terrain, topography　形成 form, become ★Using "彡" as a radical, it means shape or color.	形		
暂	② zàn *adj.* temporary; *adv.* temporarily 暂时 temporarily, for the moment ★ 暂 and 斩 have the same ending sound an.	暂		
展	① zhǎn *v.* open up, spread out 发展 develop　开展 develop, unfold　展览 exhibit	展		
值	① zhí *v.* be worth, cost 价值 value, worth　值得 deserve, be worth ★ 值 and 直 have the same pronunciation.	值		

■ 生词 NEW WORD

陡 dǒu：precipitous

■ 书写 WRITING

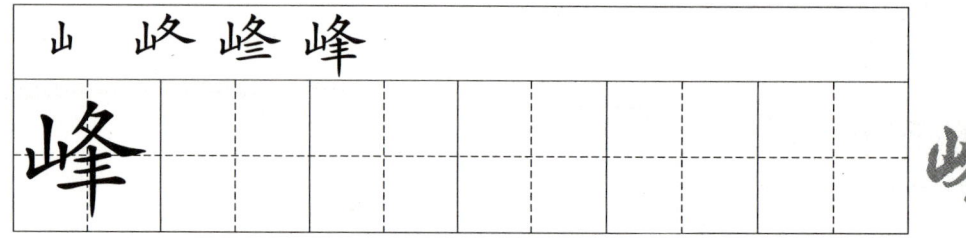

山　岖　峰　峰							
峰							

山 屮 屵 岗 岗

岗

岗

丷 凸 凸 曲 曲 曾

曾

曾

方 方 疒 旅 旅 旅

旅

旅

厶 厶 台

台

台

尸 尸 屏 屈 展 展

展

展

石

■ 课文 TEXT

拐 子

　　老李上班的时候，在公共汽车站旁看到一个人，穿着破旧的衣服、拐着左腿、眼睛里含着眼泪，旁边一台小录音机里播放着自己录的磁带："我干活时不小心打碎了老板心爱的花瓶，被砍断了腿，现在连一点儿工作的基础也没有了。请可怜可怜我吧！"地上还有一只碗，里面有一些硬币。老李觉得他的确很可怜，就在碗里也放了些硬币。

　　老李下班后，路过一家大商店的门口，又碰到了那个人，可这次，那个人拐着右腿。老李问："你上午不是说左腿被砍了吗？怎么现在变成右腿啦？"那个人说："我研究了一下，如果总是拐一只脚，这只脚上的鞋子容易磨破。"

部首 RADICAL 石 shí

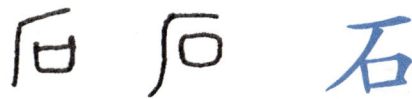

★ The character originally looked like a stone or rock falling down from the cliff. Used as a radical, it is related to stone, rock, mine, things made of stone, etc. It is usually written on the left or at the bottom.

生字 NEW CHARACTERS

课文中的石部字

砌	(礎) ① chǔ *n.* plinth 基础 base ★ 础 and 出 differ only in tone.	础		
磁	① cí *n.* magnetism; same sound as 词 磁带 tape ★ 磁 and 兹(zī) have the same ending sound -i.	磁		
砍	② kǎn *v.* chop, cut similar to 吹 and 次 ★ 砍 and 欠 have the same ending sound an.	砍		
磨	② mó *v.* grind ★ 磨 and 麻(má) have the same beginning sound m.	磨		
碰	(掽) ① pèng *v.* bump, touch; similar to 普 碰到 meet ★ Originally it meant the sound coming out when stones are rubbed or touched with each other. 碰 and 並 had similar sound in ancient times.	碰		
破	① pò *adj.* broken, damaged; similar to 坡 破旧 broken and old ★ It means "broken with a stone". 破 and 皮 have the same beginning sound p.	破		

确	(確) ① què *adj.* firm 的(dí)确 certainly, in faith　正确 correct, right ★ It is as hard as stone. 确 and 角 had similar sound in ancient times.	确		
碎	② suì *adj.* broken; *v.* break into pieces; similar to 醉 打碎 break ★It means "broken with stone". 碎 and 卒(zú) had similar sound in ancient times.	碎		
碗	① wǎn *n.* bowl [*measure word*]; same sound as 晚 一碗汤 a bowl of soup ★ The bowl was made of stone in ancient times. 碗 and 宛(wǎn) have the same pronunciation.	碗		
研	① yán *v.* grind; similar to 开; same sound as 岩 研究(jiū) research ★研 and 开(jiān) have the same ending sound ian.	研		
硬	② yìng *adj.* hard, stiff, strong same sound as 映; similar to 便 硬币 coin ★ 硬 and 更 had similar sound in ancient times.	硬		

课文中的其他生字

播	① bō *v.* seed 播放 play, televise ★ 播 and 番 (fān, pān) had similar sound in ancient times.	播		
拐	② guǎi *v.* abduct, turn; *n.* crutch, walking stick 向左拐 turn to the left　拐子 cripple, abductor ★ 拐 and 另(guǎ) have the same beginning sound g.	拐		
含	② hán *v.* keep in the mouth, contain; same sound as 寒 含泪 tears in one's eyes ★ 含 and 今 had similar sound in ancient times.	含		
泪	(淚) ② lèi *n.* tear; same sound as 累 眼泪 tear　泪水 tear ★ Water in eyes meant tears.	泪		

怜	(憐) ② lián *n.* pity, sympathy；similar to 岭 and 冷 可怜 sympathetic, pitiable, poor ★ The left part is "心". 怜 and 令 have similar sound.	怜
录	(録) ① lù *v.* copy, record same sound as 路 录音机 recorder, dictaphone	录
瓶	① píng *n.* bottle; same sound as 平 花瓶 flower vase ★ "瓦" is a radical, meaning the things are made of soil. 瓶 and 并 have the same ending sound ing.	瓶
汽	① qì *n.* steam; same sound as 气 汽车 vehicle, car ★ The vent-pipe in front of the oldest car looked like a chimney, and emits waste gas. 汽 and 气 have the same pronunciation.	汽

■ 生词 NEW WORDS

心爱 xīn'ài：beloved, treasured

断 duàn：break off

■ 书写 WRITING

石 石ˇ 矿 砬 碰 碰								碰
碰								

石 矿 碎 碎								碎
碎								

扌 扩 採 播

播

播

彐 寻 寻 录

录

录

第26课 田部 Field  26

■ 课文 TEXT

守株待兔

　　从前，有一个男人，听说山里有矿石，于是，他就在山坡上开了一块地，在那里造了一所房子，又开了几亩田，在边界上造了一堵围墙，还立了一块碑，上面写上了自己的地址和门牌号码，准备在那儿好好儿地生活。他努力奋斗，日子越过越好。

nǔ

wéi

　　平时，他还喜欢画画，这天，他拿着画好的一张画，准备去卖。走过一片森林的时候，他看到一只兔子撞到树桩上撞死了。他心里想：这世界上还真有好事让我给碰上了，看来，我的运气来了。于是，他就留在那片森林里，天天在树桩边等着，想着能再得到兔子。时间一长，不仅没能再得到兔子，连田里种的东西也都渐渐地干死了。他很后悔，说："我真傻。"这个男人忽略了一个非常重要的问题，你知道是什么吗？

shù zhuāng

shù zhuāng

147

部首 RADICAL 田 tián

★ The character originally looked like a cultivated land. Used as a radical, it is related to field, farm, etc. It is also used as a sound part.

生字 NEW CHARACTERS

课文中的田部字

备	（備）① bèi *v.* prepare similar to 各 准备 prepare	备		
奋	（奮）② fèn *v.* exert oneself; same sound as 份 奋斗 struggle ★ Originally it looked like a bird moving its wings to fly up from the field.	奋		
画	（畫）① huà *v.* describe in words, draw; *n.* painting same sound as 化 and 话 ★ The top part originally looked like a hand holding a brush, meaning delimiting a boundary.	画		
界	① jiè *n.* boundary 世界 world　边界 border ★ 界 and 介 have the same pronunciation.	界		
留	（畱）① liú *v.* stay, leave, remain; same sound as 流 留学生 overseas student ★ Originally it meant to stay in the field. 留（畱）and 罜 (liǔ) differ only in tone.	留		
略	② lüè *adj.* sketchy, brief; *n.* plan 忽略 ignore ★ Originally it meant to manage a field.	略		

亩	（畝）② mǔ *n.* a traditional unit of area (=0.0667 hectares) same sound as 母	亩		
男	① nán *n.* man, male 男人 man ★ The bottom part originally looked like a plough. It meant men should work in the field.	男		

课文中的其他生字

碑	② bēi *n.* stone stele similar to 啤 ★ 碑 and 卑(bēi) have the same pronunciation.	碑		
堵	② dǔ *n.* wall; *v.* block up; *mw* [*measure word for wall*]; similar to 都 堵车 traffic jam ★ 堵 and 者 had similar sound in ancient times.	堵		
号	（號）① hào *n.* number; háo *v.* howl 号码 number, size 记号 mark, sign ★ 号 and 丂(kǎo) have the same ending sound ɑo.	号		
悔	② huǐ *v.* regret 后悔 regret ★ 悔 and 每 have similar ending sound uei and ei.	悔		
渐	（漸）② jiàn *adv.* gradually, by degrees 渐渐地 little by little, gradually, by degrees ★ 渐 and 斩(zhǎn) have the same ending sound ɑn.	渐		
矿	（礦）② kuàng *n.* mine, mineral deposit, ore 矿泉水 mineral water 矿石 ore ★ 矿 and 广 have the same ending sound uɑng.	矿		
码	（碼）② mǎ *v.* pile up; *n.* cipher, yard 号码 number, size 码头 harbor, wharf, port, dock ★ 码 and 马 have the same pronunciation.	码		

傻	② shǎ adj. muddle-headed, stupid 傻瓜 / 傻子 fool, stupid person	傻		
址	② zhǐ n. address 地址 address ★ 址 and 止 have the same pronunciation.	址		
撞	② zhuàng v. bump against similar to 重 and 量 ★ 撞 and 童(tóng) had similar sound in ancient times.	撞		

生词 NEW WORDS

围墙 wéiqiáng：enclosing wall, enclosure

树桩 shùzhuāng：stub, stump

书写 WRITING

一 面 画 画							
画							

画

丿 ㇂ ㇂ 𰀁 留							
留							

留

石 石 矸 矹 碑 碑							
碑							

碑

口 卩 号

号 　　　　　　　　　　　　　号

亻 亻 亻 伊 伊 傻 傻

傻 　　　　　　　　　　　　　傻

■ 课文 TEXT

网络时代

　　当今，随着电脑和网络的发展，世界已经变得越来越小，国际间的交往也越来越方便。这并不是说我们生存的陆地变小了，而是说我们可以打破地理的隔离和限
制（zhì），在虚拟的空间相遇，而不管是阴天下雨还是艳阳高
照，是在大都市还是小城镇（chéng zhèn）。以前写一封信要去邮局（jú）
寄（jì），现在坐在家里，用鼠标点击一下，邮件就发出去
了。你还可以通过附件加上很多东西，比如图片等等（tú děng děng）。
如果你想找人陪你聊（liáo）天，而你的邻居（jū）又都出去郊游了，
那么，你就可以在网上寻找（xún）聊（liáo）天的对象，你不用考虑他
或她是哪个阶层（céng）的，哪怕把他或她当成是你的新郎或新
娘也没关系。这种新的通讯（xùn）方式，不仅迅速，而且也大
大降低了成本。当然，也要防止那些通过网络传（chuán）来的各
种各样的邮件，它们会给你的电脑制造很多危险（zhì wēi），除非
你在电脑上装上杀毒软件（zhuāng shā ruǎn）和防火墙，并且不断更新（duàn）。

部首 RADICAL ㄖ（阜）fù

阝 阝 阜 阝 阝

★ The character originally looked like steps on the mountain. Used as a radical, it is related to mountain, step, geography, etc. It is always written on the left and called "zuǒ'ěrpáng".

书写 WRITING

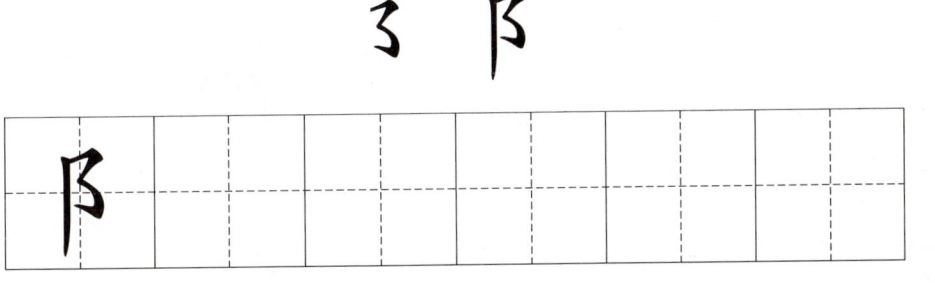

阝							

阝

生字 NEW CHARACTERS

课文中的 阝（阜）部字

除	① chú *v.* divide; *adv.* except 除非 / 除了(…以外) except, besides, but, unless ★ Originally it meant sidestep. 除 and 余 have similar ending sound u and ü.	除
防	② fáng *v.* defend, prevent; same sound as 房 防止 prevent, avoid 防火墙 fire wall, fire dam ★ The mountain protects one being attacked. 防 and 方 differ only in tone.	防
附	① fù *v.* add, attach; same sound as 富, 负 附件 attachment 附近 nearby ★It originally meant the place that was press closed. 附 and 付 have the same pronunciation.	附

153

隔	② gé　*v.* separate, cut off; same sound as 格 隔离 keep apart, segregate　隔壁 next door　隔开 separate, set apart　★ It originally meant the mountain stops one. 隔 and 鬲(gé) have the same pronunciation.	隔
际	（際）② jì　*n.* border; same sound as 计, 既, 记, 寄, 纪, 技 国际 international　★ It originally meant the border of the land. 际 and 祭(jì) have the same pronunciation.	际
陆	（陸）② lù　*n.* land, six (on checks); same sound as 录, 路 陆地 land ★ It originally meant that the mountain is on the land. 陆 and 坴(lù) have the same pronunciation.	陆
降	② jiàng　*v.* go down, fall, drop　下降 descend, go/come 　down　降低 reduce　降落伞 parachute ★ The right part originally looked like the feet stepping down (from the mountain).	降
阶	（階）② jiē　*n.* steps, stairs, rank; same sound as 接, 街 阶层 social stratum　台阶 step ★ It looks like the steps leading up on the mountain. 阶 and 介 differ only in tone.	阶
陪	② péi　*v.* accompany; same sound as 赔 陪同 accompany；companion ★ 陪 and 音(pōu) have the same beginning sound p.	陪
限	② xiàn　*v.* limit, restrict; similar to 很, 银 限制(zhì) restrict, confine, limit　无限 infinitude ★ The mountain blocks you from going out. 限 and 艮 (gèn) had the similar sound in ancient times.	限
阴	（陰）① yīn　*n.* overcast, shade 阴天 cloudy sky, overcast sky ★ It originally meant the side of the mountain with no sunshine, opposite of 阳.	阴

部首 RADICAL　阝（邑）yì

咼　吕　邑　邑　邑　阝

★ The character originally looked like a person beside
a town. Used as a radical, it is related to a place
where people live or the name of a place or a family
name. It is always written on the right and is called
"yòu'ěrpáng".

生字 NEW CHARACTERS

课文中的 阝(邑)部字

郊	② jiāo *n.* suburb 郊游 outing 郊区 suburb ★ It means an outlying part of a city or town. 郊 and 交 have the same pronunciation.	郊		
郎	② láng *n.* man 新郎 bridegroom ★ 郎 and 良 have the same beginning sound l.	郎		
邻	(鄰) ② lín *n.* neighbor; same sound as 林, 临 邻居 neighbor ★ 邻 and 令 have the similar sound.	邻		
邮	(郵) ① yóu *n.* post, mail; same sound as 油, 游 邮件 mail, post, e-mail 邮局 post office ★ It originally meant the relay station (in postal/courier system). 邮 and 由 have the same pronunciation.	邮		

课文中的其他生字

存	② cún *v.* exist, keep; similar to 在 生存 subsist, exist, live 存在 exist, be 保存 keep, save, hold ★ "子" here means the young generation that keeps the family going on.	存		
毒	③ dú *n.* poison, drug 病毒 virus 杀毒 clean the virus in computer 吸毒 take drugs 毒品 drugs	毒		
击	(擊) ② jī *v.* attack same sound as 机, 鸡 点击 click 攻击 attack	击		
件	① jiàn *mw* piece [*measure word for clothes or things*] 条 (tiáo) 件 condition 软 (ruǎn) 件 software	件		

络	(絡)③ luò　*n.* sth. resembling a net; same sound as 落 网络 network, internet　　联络 connect with ★ 络 and 各 had similar sound in ancient times.	络		
拟	(擬)④ nǐ　*v.* draft, plan; same sound as 你 虚拟 fictitious, suppositional, unreal ★ 拟 and 以 have the same ending sound i.	拟		
世	① shì　*n.* age, era, generation, life; same sound as 是, 事 世界 world　　一世 generation, whole life ★ It originally changed from "卅 (thirty)". Thirty years make one generation.	世		
虚	② xū　*n.* empty, unoccupied, false 空虚 hollow, void　　虚心 modest, reserved, open-minded ★ 虚 and 虍(hū) had similar sound in ancient times.	虚		
讯	(訊)② xùn　*n.* message; same sound as 迅 通讯 communication, message ★ 讯 and 卂 (xùn) have the same pronunciation.	讯		
艳	③(艷) yàn　*adj.* colorful, gorgeous same sound as 宴, 验 鲜艳 bright-colored, gaily-colored　　艳阳高照 sunny ★ It means "full of colors".	艳		

生词 NEW WORDS

对象 duìxiàng：target, object; boy or girl friend

新娘 xīnniáng：bride

更新 gēngxīn：rebirth, renewal, update

书写 WRITING

阝	阝	阝	阝	阝	隔			
隔								

降

存

毒

击

世

讠 讯 讯

讯 　　　　　　　　　　讯

书写以前学过的字 Writing the characters you have learned before

除 除　　　　阿 阿

队 队　　　　随 随

险 险　　　　阳 阳

院 院　　　　阵 阵

陶 陶　　　　都 都

那 那

拼音索引　*Pinyin* Index

píng	瓶	145
pō	坡	139
pó	婆	11
pò	破	143
pǔ	普	100

Q

qī	妻	11
qī	期	105
qī	欺	57
qí	崎	138
qǐ	起	87
qì	汽	145
qiǎn	浅	115
qiàn	歉	57
qiáng	墙	133
qiǎng	抢	64
qīng	清	115
qíng	情	53
qíng	晴	100
qiú	球	94
qū	岖	139
qù	趣	87
quán	泉	115
què	确	144

R

rǎn	染	116
rǎng	嚷	58

ràng	让	47
rè	热	127
rèn	认	47
rèn	任	5
róng	容	110

S

sàn	散	117
sǎng	嗓	24
sǎo	扫	64
shā	沙	116
shǎ	傻	150
shāng	伤	5
shāo	烧	128
shè	设	72
shéi	谁	48
shēn	伸	19
shēn	深	116
shèng	胜	72
shī	师	49
shī	诗	106
shī	湿	134
shí	识	47
shǐ	使	5
shǐ	始	11
shì	示	72
shì	世	156
shì	市	6
shì	试	47
shōu	收	71

shòu	受	19
shòu	瘦	18
shú	熟	128
shǔ	属	128
shǔ, shù	数	71
shuāi	摔	94
shuāng	霜	110
shuí	谁	48
shuì	睡	31
shùn	顺	36
sī	司	88
sī	思	53
sòng	送	82
sú	俗	19
sù	诉	48
sù	速	82
suí	随	49
suì	碎	144

T

tái	台	140
tái	抬	77
tán	谈	48
tán	痰	18
tǎn	坦	133
tāng	汤	116
táng	堂	134
táo	逃	82
tǎo	讨	48
tào	套	88

笔画索引　Stroke Index

阶	jiē	154
阴	yīn	154
防	fáng	153
妇	fù	10
观	guān	72

7 画

形	xíng	140
远	yuǎn	83
运	yùn	83
坏	huài	132
找	zhǎo	65
址	zhǐ	150
抓	zhuā	65
抢	qiǎng	64
坟	fén	132
抗	kàng	64
护	hù	63
块	kuài	133
拟	nǐ	156
极	jí	123
豆	dòu	36
医	yī	41
连	lián	82
坚	jiān	133
盯	dīng	30
呀	yā	58
邮	yóu	155
男	nán	149
吩	fēn	36

吹	chuī	57
吸	xī	24
吧	ba	23
岖	qū	139
岗	gāng	138
告	gào	23
估	gū	19
体	tǐ	5
何	hé	4
伸	shēn	19
伯	bó	4
住	zhù	6
位	wèi	5
伴	bàn	3
佛	fó, fú	12
近	jìn	82
希	xī	106
含	hán	144
邻	lín	155
肚	dù	39
肠	cháng	39
岛	dǎo	138
迎	yíng	83
冻	dòng	122
况	kuàng	122
亩	mǔ	149
疗	liáo	18
冷	lěng	122
闷	mēn, mèn	106
沙	shā	116

汽	qì	145
灾	zāi	128
评	píng	47
识	shí	47
诉	sù	48
词	cí	46
迟	chí	81
改	gǎi	71
际	jì	154
陆	lù	154
附	fù	153
妙	miào	11

8 画

武	wǔ	76
坦	tǎn	133
垃	lā	133
坡	pō	139
拐	guǎi	144
拖	tuō	64
顶	dǐng	35
抵	dǐ	63
抱	bào	62
拉	lā	64
拦	lán	88
拌	bàn	123
招	zhāo	65
抬	tái	77
或	huò	101
画	huà	148

哈	hā	23	浓	nóng	115	哩	lī	58
咬	yǎo	77	语	yǔ	48	啊	ā, á, ǎ,	23
科	kē	36	误	wù	48		à, a	
便	biàn	3	退	tuì	82	峰	fēng	138
顺	shùn	36	眉	méi	30	造	zào	83
保	bǎo	3	除	chú	153	敌	dí	70
促	cù	4	院	yuàn	20	透	tòu	111
俄	é	4	姨	yí	12	值	zhí	140
俗	sú	19	姻	yīn	12	倒	dǎo, dào	4
信	xìn	5	姚	yáo	12	俱	jù	13
泉	quán	115	怒	nù	77	候	hòu	4
追	zhuī	83	垒	lěi	133	倦	juàn	19
待	dài	106	络	luò	156	健	jiàn	4
须	xū	36				息	xī	54
逃	táo	82	**10 画**			途	tú	134
胧	lóng	105				爱	ài	106
胜	shèng	72	艳	yàn	156	胸	xiōng	41
胖	pàng	40	顽	wán	94	胳	gē	40
急	jí	53	赶	gǎn	87	脑	nǎo	40
弯	wān	19	起	qǐ	87	逛	guàng	82
疤	bā	17	捉	zhuō	111	留	liú	148
姜	jiāng	10	捡	jiǎn	63	恋	liàn	106
送	sòng	82	热	rè	127	准	zhǔn	122
总	zǒng	54	耻	chǐ	76	病	bìng	17
炼	liàn	127	速	sù	82	疾	jí	18
炸	zhá, zhà	128	础	chǔ	143	疼	téng	18
炮	pào	127	破	pò	143	疲	pí	18
洗	xǐ	116	套	tào	88	效	xiào	71
染	rǎn	116	顾	gù	35	凉	liáng	122
济	jì	139	顿	dùn	35	站	zhàn	59
洋	yáng	116	致	zhì	72	旅	lǚ	139

敬	jìng	71
朝	cháo, zhāo	105
逼	bī	81
硬	yìng	144
确	què	144
暂	zàn	140
悲	bēi	106
掌	zhǎng	65
晴	qíng	100
遇	yù	83
喊	hǎn	23
景	jǐng	99
跌	diē	92
跑	pǎo	93
傅	fù	12
牌	pái	77
傍	bàng	101
痛	tòng	18
普	pǔ	100
曾	céng, Zēng	139
湖	hú	115
湿	shī	134
温	wēn	111
渴	kě	123
湾	wān	140
游	yóu	116
愤	fèn	77
慌	huāng	88
愉	yú	54

寒	hán	122
遍	biàn	101
谢	xiè	48
属	shǔ	128
隔	gé	154

13 画

摸	mō	64
摆	bǎi	62
搬	bān	62
搞	gǎo	63
墓	mù	133
感	gǎn	52
碑	bēi	149
碎	suì	144
碰	pèng	143
碗	wǎn	144
雷	léi	109
零	líng	109
雾	wù	110
睛	jīng	30
瞄	miáo	31
睡	shuì	31
暖	nuǎn	100
歇	xiē	58
暗	àn	99
照	zhào	128
跨	kuà	93
路	lù	93
跳	tiào	94

跪	guì	93
跤	jiāo	93
跟	gēn	93
嗓	sǎng	24
愁	chóu	106
傻	shǎ	150
像	xiàng	5
躲	duǒ	83
腰	yāo	41
腿	tuǐ	40
痰	tán	18
意	yì	54
数	shǔ, shù	71
煎	jiān	127
煤	méi	127
满	mǎn	115
源	yuán	117
媳	xí	11
嫁	jià	10

14 画

熬	áo	126
墙	qiáng	133
境	jìng	133
摔	shuāi	94
歌	gē	57
磁	cí	143
愿	yuàn	54
需	xū	110
颗	kē	35